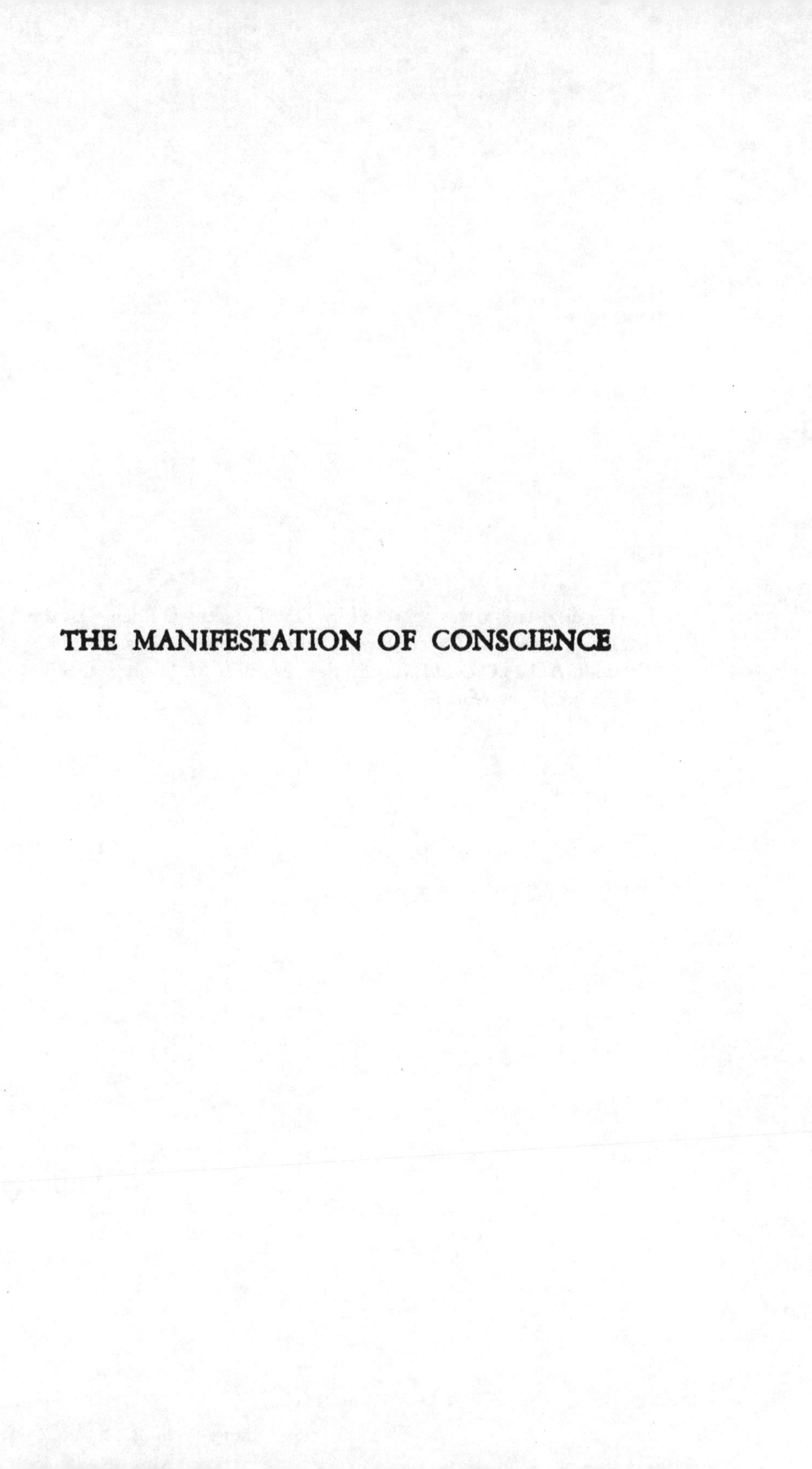

THE MANIFESTATION OF CONSCIENCE

This dissertation was approved by Rev. Romaeus O'Brien, O. Carm., J.C.D., professor of Canon Law, as director and by Rev. John Rogg Schmidt, A.B., J.C.D., LL.B. and Rev. Meletius M. Wojnar, O.S.B.M., S.T.L., J.C.D. as readers.

THE CATHOLIC UNIVERSITY OF AMERICA
CANON LAW STUDIES
NO. 410

THE MANIFESTATION OF CONSCIENCE

A DISSERTATION

Submitted to the Faculty of the School of Canon Law of The Catholic University of America in Partial Fulfillment of the Requirements for the Degree of Doctor of Canon Law

BY

Rev. Dacian Dee, O.F.M. Cap., B.A., J.C.L.
PRIEST OF THE NEW YORK PROVINCE OF SAINT MARY

THE CATHOLIC UNIVERSITY OF AMERICA PRESS
WASHINGTON, D.C.
1960

Nihil Obstat:

JORDANUS SULLIVAN, O.F.M. CAP., J.C.D.
Censor Deputatus

Garrisonii, die 7 martii, 1960.

Imprimi Potest:

SERAPHINUS WINTERROTH, O.F.M. CAP.
Minister Provincialis

Providentiae, die 9 martii, 1960.

Nihil Obstat:

ROMAEUS O'BRIEN, O. CARM., J.C.D.
Censor Deputatus

Washingtonii, die 18 martii, 1960.

Imprimatur:

✠PATRICIUS A. O'BOYLE
Archiepiscopus Washingtoniensis

Washingtonii, die 19 martii, 1960.

PRINTED BY
THE CAPUCHIN PRESS
PITTSBURGH, PENNSYLVANIA

SAINT LAWRENCE OF BRINDISI, CAPUCHIN PRIEST AND DOCTOR OF THE UNIVERSAL CHURCH

FOREWORD

The manifestation of conscience is a complex institution bringing into focus historical, canonical, moral and ascetical elements. The present study does not portend to cover all these factors. By its nature this work is historico-canonical, and while at times the realm of the moral is of necessity entered upon, a studied effort has been made to avoid the numerous ascetical considerations related to the manifestation of conscience.

The historical evolution of the manifestation is traced from the beginnings of Christianity down to the present day. Since the basic development of the manifestation of conscience took place between the third and seventeenth centuries, this period is given greater attention than are the more recent centuries. The juridical recognition and regulation of the manifestation of conscience was a process of three inter-related stages. The first of these finds its expression in the relevant norms of various Religious Rules and Constitutions. The final two stages are expressions of the common law itself, namely, the decree *Quemadmodum* of 1890 and canon 530 of the Code. The present law of the Church as regards the manifestation of conscience is canon 530. It is this law, therefore, which receives paramount consideration in the canonical part of the present work. The decree *Quemadmodum,* however, is the historical and legal basis for the canon, and as such must receive frequent and relatively detailed examination. Hence the canonical chapters of this work consist mainly of a commentary on canon 530 as the outgrowth of and climax to the decree *Quemadmodum,* the first common law to give particularized attention to the manifestation of conscience.

The writer wishes to take this occasion to thank his Capuchin Superiors, Provincial and local, Very Rev. Fathers Seraphin Winterroth and Lambert Roessner of the Province of Saint Mary, and Very Rev. Fathers Giles Staab, Claude Vogel, Rt. Rev. Monsignor Firmin Schmidt and Rev. Father Stephen Rowe of the Province of Saint Augustine, for the opportunity of persuing advanced studies in canon law. Likewise he wishes to thank the Canon Law Faculty of the Catholic University of America for their kind and helpful assistance over the past three years, and in particular Rev. Romaeus O'Brien, O. Carm., the director of this dissertation. Finally the writer expresses his thanks to his classmates and confreres for their assistance and encouragement, especially to the Capuchin Fathers Myles Schmitt and Jordan Sullivan for their valuable suggestions and Sebastian Falcone and Leonard Glavin for many helps in bringing this work to its present final form.

TABLE OF CONTENTS

CANONICAL COMMENTARY

Chapter IV

Chapter V

Chapter VI

CHAPTER I

BEGINNINGS AND EARLY DEVELOPMENT OF THE MANIFESTATION OF CONSCIENCE

ARTICLE 1: HISTORICAL EVOLUTION OF THE MANIFESTATION UP TO 500 A.D.

The manifestation of conscience has always been closely linked with the practice of spiritual direction in the religious life. It is natural therefore that the first references to the manifestation should be found in the early Religious Rules and in the writings of the first proponents of the religious life. Of necessity many of these early references are but vague suggestions of the present precise concept of the manifestation. Nevertheless, the beginnings of this present concept are easily recognized in the passages from these ancient Rules and writings which are examined in the present chapter.

Section 1: *Testimony of St. Anthony the Great* (251?-356)

St. Anthony the Great retired completely into the desert about the year 285 and gave himself up to a life of asceticism. Since the holiness and ordered discipline of his life attracted a number of disciples, the saint is known as the founder of the eremitic form of religious life.[1] The writings of St. Anthony contain the first suggestions of what was to develop into the present, more defined concept of the manifestation of conscience.

The first reference occurs in the *Regulae ac Praecepta S.P.N. Antonii ad Filios Suos Monachos:* "Do not open your thoughts to all men but only to those who are able to save your souls."[2] Rule XLI of the Arabic translation of these *Regulae* contains a similar admonition: "You are not

[1] "Saint Anthony the Great," *The Oxford Dictionary of the Christian Church* (London: Oxford University Press, 1957), p. 65 (hereafter cited *Oxford Dictionary*).

[2] "Ne propales cogitationes tuas cunctis hominibus, sed solum iis qui possunt salvare animam tuam." — Migne, *Patrologiae Cursus Completus, Series Graeca* (161 vols., Parisiis, 1856-1866), XL, col. 1070, (hereafter cited *MPG*); Holstensius-Brockie, *Codex Regularum Monasticarum et Canonicarum* (6 vols., Augustae Vindelicorum, 1759), I, 4, (hereafter cited *CR*).

to open your thoughts to all but only to those who are able to save your soul."[3] A third pertinent reference is found in the *Epistolae Viginti S.P.B. Antonii Magni Monachorum*. Letter XVIII of this series exhorts the monk to seek the assistance of another in time of spiritual illness:

> Thus the soul of man, unless the joy of God be in it, will be sick and break open in bad wounds. But if it will seek out some minister of God who is skilled in the healing of the spirit, and will cling to him, he will free the soul from its passions and will raise it up again and will teach it of God, and it will obtain that joy which is its food. Then, indeed, will it [the soul of man] be able to withstand the enemies which are the spirits of evil, and will conquer them and trample them under foot with their counsels and be filled with joy...[4]

St. Anthony recognizes the need of opening one's heart to another if progress is to be made in the spiritual life. This guide must be skilled and experienced in things of the spirit, for only such a man is worthy to know the secrets of the heart and can properly direct the one confiding in him.

Although the saint stresses the importance of revealing one's thoughts to a competent spiritual guide, he refrains from forcing his followers into this practice. Tangible proof that the ultimate decision rested with the individual ascetic is found in the incident of the *Tres Seniores:*

> Three elders were accustomed to come to the blessed abbot Anthony each year, and two of these consulted him about their thoughts and the salvation of their souls. The third, however, was always silent and doubted about nothing. After much time the abbot Anthony said to him: 'How is it that for a long time now you have been coming to me, and yet you ask me nothing?' He answered: 'For me, Father, it is sufficient to see you.'[5]

[3] "Cogitationes tuas omnibus ne aperias sed iis tantum qui animam tuam salvare possunt."—*Sanctissimi Patris Nostri Antonii Magni Abbatis Regulae sive Canones, ad Filios Monachos, Ex Arabico, interprete Abrahamo Ecchellensi, MPG,* XL, col. 1065.

[4] "Sic hominis anima, nisi Dei gaudium illi insit, infirmabitur, et mala in vulnera incidit. Si vero quaerere conabitur hominem aliquem Dei ministrum spiritualis peritum medicinae, illique adhaerebit; is illam primum sanabit a passionibus, iterumque resurget, eamque Dei causa erudiet, et obtinebit gaudium illud quod est illius alimentum; tum vero hostibus obsistere poterit qui sunt spiritus mali, eosque superabit et conculcabit eorum consilia, et gaudio perficietur..."—*MPG,* XL, col. 1048.

[5] "Tres seniores singulis annis semel proficisci solebant ad B. Abbatem Antonium, e quibus duo illum de suis cogitationibus et animarum salute consulebat; tertius vero silebat perpetuo, et de nulla contabatur re. Post multum autem temporis ait illi abbas Antonius: 'Iamdiu ad me venis, et de nulla re me interrogas?' Respondit: 'Sufficit mihi, Pater mi, te videre'."—*MPG,* XL, cols. 1098-1099.

Section 2: Testimony of St. Basil the Great (c. 330-379)

St. Basil, whose name is associated with the beginnings of Greek monasticism, composed his religious Rule in the years 358-364. The far-reaching wisdom embodied in this Rule still makes it the basis of monastic practice in the Eastern Church. His Rule assumes two forms, the *Regulae fusius tractatae*,[6] and the *Regulae brevius tractatae*.[7] In both forms of his Rule St. Basil follows the question and answer method of exposition. While it is strict, the Rule of St. Basil does not encourage the extreme austerities of the hermits of the desert. It conceives of asceticism as a means to the perfect service of God, to be achieved in community life under obedience.[8]

There are a number of relevant passages in this double Rule of St. Basil. Question XXVI of the *Regulae fusius tractatae*, for example, contains the first clear statement of a manifestation of faults for the sake of direction:

> Any one of the subjects, if he wish to make exceeding progress and be spent in the precepts of our Lord Jesus Christ and be in a firm and stable state, must keep to himself neither hidden movements of soul nor any inconsiderate word uttered, but rather he is to open his heart's secrets to these brethren who are in charge of caring kindly and humanly for the sick. In this way whatever is laudable is made firm, and on the other hand, whatever is reprehensible is cured by a fitting remedy. Through this exercise perfection will be gained by us, as improvement is gradually made.[9]

Question XLIV of the same *Regulae* speaks of travels and makes provisions for the account which the monk is to render on his return to the monastery. It might be noted, parenthetically, that this same passage is cited by Suarez in his extensive treatment of the manifestation

[6] *MPG*, XXXI, cols. 890-1051.

[7] *MPG*, XXXI, cols. 1051-1306.

[8] "Rule of Saint Basil," *Oxford Dictionary*, p. 139.

[9] "Unusquisque autem eorum qui subditi sunt, si modo profectum eximium velit facere, et in ejus vitae quae ex Domini nostri Jesu Christi praeceptis transigitur, firmo et stabili statu versari, debet neque motum ullum animae occultum apud seipsum servare, neque verbum ullum inconsiderate proferre, sed hisce fratribus, qui infirmis benigne et humane curandis praefecti sunt, cordis arcana aperire. Ita enim quod laudabile est, stabilitur, quod vero reprobum, congruenti remedio sanabitur: atque per mutuum hujusmodi exercitium perfectio a nobis comparabitur, facta paulatim accessione."—*MPG*, XXXI, cols. 986-987.

of conscience.[10] The selection from St. Basil reads:

> The prefect, upon the return of the traveler, is to question him as to what he has done, into what assemblies of men he has come, what exchange of words he has had with them, what has taken place in his soul, whether he was in the fear of God throughout the entire day and night, whether he was guilty of violating any of those things set down—either because he was overcome by external trials, or because he yielded through his own sloth.
>
> With regard to those things he has done well he is to be confirmed by praise. But with regard to those things in which he was wanting, the prefect is to correct him by diligent exhortation.[11]

In Question CCXXVI of the *Regulae brevius tractatae* St. Basil again takes up the revelation of internal matters:

> Is it necessary that one reveal to others those things which he feels; or having convinced himself that something which he has done is pleasing to God, should he keep it to himself?[12]

By way of answer the saint says in effect that we are to reveal these matters to those who, sharing our same interests, are solid in faith and prudence, so as to be corrected where we have erred and to be encouraged in those instances in which we have acted laudably.[13] The manner in which the saint formulates his answer suggests that he sets small value on the subject's personal judgment in matters so intimate. As a result, he stresses the importance and advantages of such self-revelation and the reliance on the judgment of one more experienced.

[10]*Opera Omnia* (Editio Nova, a Carolo Berton, Parisiis: Apud Ludovicum Vives, 1877), XVI bis, 1083.

[11]"Caeterum praefectus post reditum viatorem percontetur, quid egerit, in quorum hominum venerit congressum, quos cum eis sermones habuerit, quid versaverit animo, num diem totamque noctem exegerit in timore Dei, an praevaricatus sit, et aliquid violaverit eorum quae statuta sunt, aut externis incommodis victus, aut sua segnitie dilapsus.

"Et quod quidem recte gestum est, laudando confirmet: in quo vero deliquit, id corrigat diligenti ac perita adhortatione."—*MPG*, XXXI, cols. 1030-1031.

[12]"Utrum oporteat unumquemque ea quae sentit, aliis patefacere: an cum sibi persuasum fuerit, rem quae geritur, Deo esse gratam, eam debeat apud seipsum continere."—*MPG*, XXXI, col. 1234.

[13]"Memores sententiae Dei, qui dixit per prophetam ... communicare nos res nostras cum iis qui nobis conjunctissimi sunt, quisque tum fidei tum prudentiae specimen dederunt, necesse esse arbitramur: ut aut quod erroneum est, corrigatur, aut quod recte factum est stabiliatur, sicque effugiamus nos memoratum jam judicium, quod adversum eos qui in seipsis prudentes sunt, prolatum est."—*Loc. cit.*

Holstensius-Brockie do not divide St. Basil's Rule into the *Regulae fusius tractatae* and the *Regulae brevius tractatae,* but simply designate it the *Regulae Sancti Basilii Episcopi Cappadociae ad Monachos.* Question CC of this version asks: "If evil things have been done, should one make confession to all or only to certain ones, and to which of these?"[14] St. Basil answers that the confession of sins in question is like the disclosure of an illness to a doctor. Just as bodily wounds are not revealed to everyone but only to those who possess specialized skill and knowledge of cures, so, likewise, the confession of sins must be made only to those who have the competence to care for and improve the sinner.[15]

If this passage of St. Basil refers to sacramental confession, it offers no evidence to the present work. Two cogent considerations, however, indicate that by the word *confessio* St. Basil was referring rather to a non-sacramental manifestation. In the first place, the point and purpose of Question CC vanish on the assumption that the saint is speaking of sacramental confession, because he is specifically inquiring about the necessity of confession to all. It is an absurd hypothesis to argue that St. Basil was willing to concede the power of absolution to everyone. This argument assumes added weight in view of the fact that in St. Basil's time the majority of monks were not priests. Secondly, the word *confessio* as used in earlier centuries had a broader connotation than its present, technical meaning would allow. In one of its most recurrent usages it designated a non-sacramental manifestation of faults. This point will be demonstrated in a later section of the present chapter.[16]

St. Basil, like St. Anthony, stresses the importance of opening one's heart for the sake of direction. Progress in the spiritual life is impossible without the help of an experienced guide. The effectiveness of this guide is seriously limited unless he knows the innermost feelings of his charges. Therefore, subjects are to open their hearts to their spiritual fathers. A new element is introduced in the testimony of St. Basil.

[14]"Si oporteat gesta turpia vel obscoena confitentem inverecundius pronunciare omnibus, aut certis quibusque, et quibus illis?"—*CR,* I, 107.

[15]"Confessio peccatorum hanc habet rationem quam habet vulnus aliquod corporis vel passio, quae medico demonstranda est. Sicut ergo non omnibus quis vitia vel vulnera corporis sui revelat, nec quibuslibet, sed his tantummodo, qui summae peritiae testimonium habent, et curae ac medelae disciplinam; ita et confessio peccatorum fieri debet apud eos tantummodo, qui curare haec praevalent ac mendare . . ." —*Loc. cit.*

[16]Cf. *infra,* pp. 13-14.

When the traveler returns home, he is to be questioned by the prefect even as to "what has taken place in his soul." For the first time the incentive regarding internal revelations is committed to the superior rather than to the subject.

Section 3: Testimony of Isaias the Abbot (fl. 372)

There is some question as to whether Isaias actually wrote the Rule which has been associated with his name throughout the centuries.[17] In spite of the doubt about its authorship,[18] this Rule is included here because of its antiquity and its incorporation in the classical works of both Migne and Holstensius-Brockie.

Rule VI of the *Regulae ad Monachos* contains at least a suggestion of the manifestation of internal matters to others. It reads: "Reveal your problems to your fathers that you might receive help through their counsels."[19] Later sections of the same *Regula* offer more precise references to the revealing of one's thoughts for the sake of direction. Rule XLII states:

> If you consult any elder concerning your thoughts, open them freely and exactly to him . . . ; nor are you to take special account of him who is of advanced age, but rather select him who is accomplished in doctrine, practice, and spiritual experience, lest you suffer harm and your passions mount in intensity.[20]

Rule LXV contains a similar admonition: "Concerning no other matter

[17]"Eodem hoc tempore floruit s. Isaias (Esaias) abbas in eremo scietico (fl. c. 372), cui tribuuntur orationes XXIX, capitula XXX *de religiosa exercitatione et quiete*, ex illis orationibus excerpta; praecepta LXVIII seu *consilia* posita tironibus in monachatu. Juxta alios tamen hac tribuenda sunt Isaiae ascetae, qui decessisse dicitur intra a. 485-490."—Hurter, *Nomenclator Literarius Theologiae Catholicae* (6 vols., 3. ed. Oeniponte, Libraria Academica Wagneriana, 1903-1913), I, 227.

[18]Cf. Steiger, "De Propagatione et Diffusione Vitae Religiosae. Synopsis Historica,"—*Periodica,* XIII (1924), (55).

[19]"Aperi morbos tuos patribus tuis, ut experias opem per ipsorum consilium."—Migne, *Patrologiae Cursus Completus, Series Latina* (221 vols., Parisiis, 1844-1864), CIII, col. 429 (hereafter cited *MPL*); *CR,* I, 6.

[20]"Si quem senem interrogaveris de cogitationibus tuis, aperi illas libere uti se habeant ei quem tua arcana servaturum confidis; nec rationem habeas illius, qui provectae aetatis est, sed qui doctrina, opere, et spirituali experimento pollet, ne referas damnum, si augeantur passiones tuae."—*MPL,* CIII, col. 431; *CR,* I, 9.

do the devils so rejoice as they do over him who conceals his thoughts from his spiritual master."[21]

These selections from the Rule of Isaias confirm the basic position already taken by Sts. Anthony and Basil in their recognition of the spiritual advantages accruing from the practice of self-revelation. Isaias adds a new note by cautioning subjects to exercise great prudence in their choice of confidant. For the first time special emphasis is placed upon the qualifications which must characterize the recipient of the monk's spiritual secrets.

Section 4: *Testimonies of Evagrius Ponticus* (346-399) *and St. Jerome* (342-420)

These two ecclesiastical writers are included in the present historical survey only insofar as they offer confirmatory evidence. Neither Evagrius nor St. Jerome adds a further dimension to the practice of the manifestation, but both re-echo and endorse the recommendations proffered by earlier spiritual masters.

Evagrius, a native of Pontus, retired to the Nitrian desert in 382. His is the distinction of being the first monk to have done extensive writing.[22] Among the *Evagrii Monachi Sententiae*[23] is found the following clear reference to self-revelation orientated towards spiritual advancement:

> Hear, O monk, the words of your father, and do not make his instructions ineffectual. When he sends for you, obey him and commit to him your thoughts; for in this way you will fly from evil thoughts and the evil demons will not prevail against you.[24]

The wisdom here embodied, and indeed the choice of terminology, run parallel to the related contributions of St. Basil and Isaias the Abbot.

[21]"De nulla re ita laetantur diaboli, sicuti laetantur de eo, qui cogitationes suas spiritualem suum magistrum celat."—*MPL*, CIII, 434; *CR*, I, 9.

[22]"Evagrius Ponticus," *Oxford Dictionary*, p. 476.

[23]This is not a Regula in the strict sense. Holstensius-Brockie place it in an appendix to Vol. I of the *Codex Regularum* among the *Exhortationes SS. Patrum ad Monachos et Virgines*.—*CR*, I, 465-468; *MPG*, XL, col. 1280.

[24]"Audi, monache, sermones patris tui, et ne irritas facias eruditiones ejus. Cum miserit te, obaudi ei, et quantum ad mentem comitere cum eo; hoc enim modo effugies cogitationes malas, et maligni daemones non praevalebunt adversum te."—*CR*, I, 466; *MPG*, XL, 1280.

It is sufficient to consider that, like St. Basil,[25] Evagrius assigns to the elder the initiative of summoning the spiritual disciple. Moreover, like Isaias,[26] he threatens diabolical victory as the consequence of concealing one's thoughts from his spiritual father.

St. Jerome, whose intellectual excellence has unfortunately been associated solely with his scriptural scholarship, had frequent occasion to write on the religious life. Although he never authored a Rule[27] nor even gave systematic consideration to monastic institutes, he did touch at least on one occasion upon the subject of present interest. In Letter CXXV he expresses the conviction that the cenobitic form of religious life affords greater spiritual advantages than its eremitic counterpart. He explains that life in a monastery makes available to the individual religious a leader and guide who is familiar with the path along which he has never ventured. In this way, the subject will be safeguarded from the danger of wandering or delaying, and will be cautioned against too rapid or too leisurely a pace.[28]

The saint is primarily concerned with a practical guarantee of steady and efficient progress in the spiritual life. He finds this guarantee personified in an experienced guide to whom one may open his heart and thereby receive proper direction.

Section 5: *Testimony of John Cassian* (c. 360-435)

John Cassian was an Eastern monk who emigrated to the West, and in the early fifth century founded two monasteries near Marseilles.[29] His writings offer a more thorough treatment of the manifestation within the lines set down by previous writers. In addition, he makes an

[25]Cf. *supra*, pp. 4-6.

[26]Cf. *supra*, pp. 6-7.

[27]"Nullam edidit regulam, tametsi sub ejus nomine quaedam circumfertur."—Steiger, "De Propagatione et Diffusione Vitae Religiosae. Synopsis Historica," *Periodica*, XIII (1924), (74).

[28]"Primumque tractandum est, utrum solus, an cum aliis in monasterio vivere debeas. Mihi quidem placet, ut habeas Sanctorum contubernium nec ipse te doceas, et absque ductore ingrediaris viam, quam nunquam ingressus es, statimque tibi in partem alteram declinandum sit, et errori pateas, plusque aut minus ambules, quam necesse est; ne aut currens lasseris aut moram faciens, abdormias."—*MPL*, XXII, col. 1077.

[29]"John Cassian," *Oxford Dictionary*, p. 243.

original contribution by focusing attention on the obligation of secrecy which binds the recipients of the manifestation.

In *De Institutis* Cassian points to simplicity and frankness with spiritual elders as a sign of true humility:

> By these signs humility can be proved: first, if one mortifies his own preferences in all things; second, if he conceals neither his actions nor even his thoughts from his elder; third, if he leaves nothing to his own discretion but commits everything to the judgment of his elder and listens with eagerness to the latter's exhortations.[30]

In another setting Cassian again traces the relationship between humility and spiritual self-revelation. In *Collatio II* his thoughts on discretion are delivered through a certain Abbot Moses. Discretion, he explains, is not acquired independently of true humility. The foremost test of this humility consists in a series of three gradient acts: revelation of thoughts to spiritual elders, acquiescence in their judgments, acceptance of their decisions as a practical norm of action.[31]

In the course of the same discussion Cassian declares that the devil's most successful snare is spiritual self-reliance with its attendant neglect of the advice of elders. The nature of the spiritual life, by reason of its transcendence over all other human disciplines as well as the eternal definitiveness of its goal, absolutely postulates the services of a competent spiritual guide. Therefore, Cassian urges the religious to make an unqualified manifestation to spiritual elders and to accept reverently the advice they offer.[32]

30"Humilitas vero his indiciis comprobatur: primo si mortificatas sese omnes habeat voluntates, secundo si non solum suorum actuum, verum etiam cogitationum nihil suum celaverit seniorem, tertio si nihil suae discretioni, sed iudicio eius universa committat ac monita eius sitiens ac liberanter auscultet."—*MPL,* XLIX, col. 199.

31"Tum Moyses: Vera, inquit, discretio non nisi vera humilitate acquiritur. Cuius humilitatis haec erit prima probatio si universa non solum quae cogitantur, seniorum reserventur examini, ut nihil suo quis iudicio credens illorum per omnia definitionibus adquiescat et quid bonum vel malum debeat iudicare eorum traditione cognoscat."—*MPL,* XLIX, 537.

32"Nullo namque alio vitio tam praecipitem diabolus monachum pertrahit ac perducit ad mortem, quam cum eum neglectus consiliis seniorum suo iudicio persuaserit definitionique confidere. Etenim cum omnes artes ac disciplinae humano ingenio repertae et quae nihil amplius quam vitae hujus temporariae commodis prosunt, licet manu palpari queant et oculis pervideri, recte tamen a quoquam sine instituentis doctrina nequeant comprehendi, quam ineptum est credere hanc solam non egere doctore, quae et invisibilis et occulta est et quae non nisi corde purissimo

The most important contribution of John Cassian lies in the emphasis he placed upon the secrecy which must accompany the manifestation. By way of explicit reference to an unfortunate incident which took place in Syria, he reminds spiritual elders of the special secrecy which attaches to their office. He further warns these spiritual guides against the evil consequences which arise from a violation of this secrecy.[33] Thus, as early as the fifth century, there was a marked awareness of the necessity of unquestioned confidence as a fundamental pre-requisite for the manifestation of conscience. The burden of cultivating such trustworthiness Cassian placed upon the shoulders of the spiritual masters. Without a doubt the introduction of this reciprocal element represents the development of the manifestation into a more defined institution.

Section 6: *Testimony of Isaias the Abbot* (fl. 488)

Migne edits the writings of another Isaias the Abbot,[34] a monk who flourished more than a hundred years later than the prelate of the same name considered under Section 3. In his *Oratio I* Isaias enjoins upon the monks the revelation of their state of soul to the abbot for the purpose of guidance: "Do not conceal your thoughts, afflictions, and suspicions, but indicate all of them to your abbot, and accept with confidence whatever he may have to offer."[35] A later section, namely, *Oratio VI,* likewise, contains a direct reference to the practice of self-revelation. Here it is clearly indicated that the inner state of the soul is not to be disclosed to everyone. For such confidences are to be reserved

---

pervidetur, cuius error non temporale damnum nec quod facile reparatur, sed animae perditionem parit mortemque perpetuam . . . Et ideo semper seniorum summa cautione sunt sectanda vestigia atque ad eos cuncta quae in nostris cordibus oriuntur sublato confusionis velamine deferanda."—*MPL,* XLIX, cols. 541-542.

[33]"Occasionem nobis perniciosae verecundiae, qua cogitationes malas studeamus obtegere, illa praecipue creat causa, qua novimus quendam in Syriae partibus, ut credebatur, praecipuum seniorum cuidam fratri cogitationes suas simplici confessione prodenti postmodum quadam indignatione commotum easdem graviter exprobasse. Unde fit, ut dum eas in nobis premimus ac senioribus erubescimus publicare, curationum remedia consequi nequeamus."—*MPL,* XLIX, col. 542.

[34]Cf. *supra,* pp. 6-7.

[35]"Cogitationes et afflictiones et suspiciones vestras nolite abscondere, sed eas abbati vestro cunctas indicate; et quod ab ipso auditis, id cum fide percipite."—*MPG,* XL, col. 1107.

for one's director—lest the heart become weary with sadness.[36] Finally, in *Oratio VIII* Isaias prohibits the revealing of mind and will to the ignorant and imprudent. Evidently, the implication is that only the wise and prudent are qualified to receive such intimate manifestations of the spirit.[37]

While the testimony of Isaias the Abbot does not furnish a truly new insight into the manifestation of conscience, its value is not to be underestimated. His expressions, on the one hand, are strongly redolent of the thought, language, and wisdom of St. Anthony the Great of Egypt,[38] and, on the other, he leaves no doubt as to the necessity of restricting all spiritual disclosures only to duly qualified persons. Perhaps the point of significance in Isaias the Abbot is that his concern with the qualifications of the recipients is an indication that the manifestation of conscience by this time had already become a fairly standardized practice in monastic circles.

Section 7: *Ordo Monasticus in Veteri Scotiae Monasterio de Kilros olim Observatus* (5th Century)

In their comprehensive editions of the early monastic Rules, both Migne and Holstensius-Brockie include the so-called *Rule of Life of the Ancient Scot Monastery of Kilros*. Both assign the date of composition to the 5th Century.

The relevant passage from this Rule prescribes that the monks scrutinize their innermost hearts at an appointed time each day. At the conclusion of this exercise they are to present themselves to their spiritual father in order to manifest to him the results of their soul-searching. A final exhortation urges them to be completely docile to the salutary counsels and commands of the spiritual father.[39]

[36]"Cogitationes tuas noli quibuslibet aperire, sed patribus tantum tuis, ne tristitiam contrahas in corde tuo."—*MPG*, XL, col. 1126.

[37]"Noli mentem tuam ignorantibus aperire, nec voluntatem tuam imprudentibus patefacere."—*MPG*, XL, col. 1131.

[38]Cf. *supra*, p. 2.

[39]"... excepta una hora post matutinas laudes, quando sese ad scrutanda intima cordis secreta praeparabant. Qua peracta, et vere compuncti, patrem spiritualem accesserunt, cui cogitationes suas propalabant, sine cujus jussu nihil praestare potuerunt, sed illius licentiam etiam vel ad naturae requisita acquirebant."—*MPL*, LIX, col. 565; *CR*, II, 64.

The importance of this testimony is based upon two considerations. First, by the fifth century the manifestation of conscience was a recognized practice in a monastic foundation beyond the pale of the Roman Empire. Second, there is a provision made here for intimate spiritual consultation on a daily basis.

Conclusion

From the first five centuries of Christianity, shreds of evidence, disparate and scattered, can be pieced together to prove that the revelation of conscience to religious superiors and elders was not only an accomplished fact, but also that in a relatively short time it crystallized into an approved and even highly recommended spiritual practice. In fact, recognition of the spiritual values inherent in such confidential revelations is, for all effects and purposes, coincident with the beginnings of the religious life.

Already under *St. Anthony the Great,* this ascetical practice is clearly ascertained. A general need for prudence is underlined, and a number of spiritual advantages (e.g., individualized instruction, effective repression of passions, joy) are mentioned in an incidental way. *St. Basil* sees in this practice a favorable condition for rapid spiritual growth, because it provides an incentive for greater generosity towards God, or, if need be, a corrective for unsuitable deeds. The patriarch of Eastern monasticism, more than any other writer of this period, heightens the role of the spiritual guide. This can only result in a corresponding de-emphasis on the merits of personal judgment in ascetical efforts. Which is indeed the case. The earlier *Isaias the Abbot* is for the most part preoccupied with the qualifications which those singled out for such confidences of the spirit must possess. The writings of *Evagrius Ponticus* and *St. Jerome* in this connection are of relatively minor importance. The latter, however, not without reason describes spiritual self-disclosure in function of a reliable gauge for ascetical progress. *John Cassian,* from a relative standpoint, traces the points of contact between the manifestation of the spirit and the acquisition of the virtue of humility. From an absolute viewpoint, he singles out for special consideration the secrecy which must surround and safeguard these revelations of the interior life. The second *Isaias the Abbot,* not unlike the first, is primarily interested in determining the traits which the recipients of the manifestation must have. The *Rule of Life of the Monastery of Kilros* provides a special place in the daily schedule of self-evaluation and consultation with a spiritual guide.

It may be noted that these early writers not only encouraged the manifestation of the spirit, but some, for instance St. Basil and the later Isaias the Abbot, were so convinced of its efficacy that they even enjoined it upon their followers.

Article 2: Historical Evolution of the Manifestation from 500-1000

Section 1: *Testimony of St. Benedict* (c. 480-c. 550)

St. Benedict has justly been designated the Patriarch of Western Monasticism, because of the deep-rooted influence exerted by his Rule on subsequent monastic legislation. This Rule embodies a number of references to the manifestation of secret actions and thoughts. In the Seventh Chapter, for example, St. Benedict writes:

> This is the fifth degree of humility: by humble confession not to conceal from the abbot any evil thoughts that enter into the heart nor the evil deeds one has secretly committed.[40]

This passage unmistakably calls for a manifestation of conscience. It should be noted that the saint here speaks of "humble confession" made to the abbot. Is this to be interpreted as a sacramental confession, or merely as a non-sacramental manifestation of conscience? Suarez takes up the problem involved and concludes that St. Benedict does not intend a sacramental revelation. He explains that the saint himself was not a priest and that the abbots of the period were usually not priests. Consequently, this disclosure of evil thoughts and actions to be made to the abbot could only be a non-sacramental manifestation of conscience.[41]

Cuthbert Butler, O.S.B., an acknowledged authority on the history of monasticism, draws the same conclusion:

> There is here no question of sacramental confession; in those days the abbot was not commonly a priest; it is doubtful whether Saint

[40]"Quintus humilitatis gradus est, si omnes cogitationes malas cordi suo advenientes vel mala a se absconse commissa per humilem confessionem abbatem non celavit suum."—*MPL,* LXVI, col. 589; *CR,* I, 120.

[41]"Et quamvis ibi Turrecremata de confessione sacramentali locum illum intelligere videatur, tamen, si quis consideret ipsummet S. Benedictum sacerdotem non fuisse, et illo tempore Abbates ordinarie non fuisse presbyteros, facile intelliget Benedictum non limitare illud consilium ad sacramentalem confessionem."—Suarez, *Opera Omnia,* XVI bis, 1083-1084.

> Benedict was. The object in view was simply self-discipline and guidance.[42]

Dom Delatte's classic commentary on the Benedictine Rule fully confirms this conclusion:

> Is our Holy Father here contrasting public confession of faults against the Rule, and penance for such, with secret confession of theological faults? More probably he refers to an extrasacramental manifestation ... The brother with filial purpose and loyal desire to amend, should manifest his state candidly—not to the whole community ... but to the abbot or spiritual seniors .... So we shall tell the abbot even though he look austere and we fear his judgment and the results of our confidences ... Has he not a right to know what is going on in his house and in his monks?[43]

The weight of extrinsic authority, in addition to intrinsic considerations, leave no doubt that the *confession* here spoken of is a non-sacramental manifestation of evil thoughts and secret actions.

A second reference occurs in Chapter Forty-Six of the same Rule. The saint first speaks of public faults and indicates that these are to be made known to the abbot or in the Chapter. He then proceeds to hidden and internal faults and states that these are to be revealed only to the abbot and spiritual elders, because these alone are capable of providing suitable remedies. In this passage the legislator also makes reference to the obligation of secrecy incumbent upon directors of the spirit.[44]

St. Benedict adds a new note in Chapter Forty-Nine of the Rule. Whereas his previous references were concerned with the acknowledgment of faults, the present text deals with the revelation of promptings to a more austere and holy life. He explains that whenever one is prompted to go beyond the ordinary prescriptions of the Rule, he must first submit the matter to the judgment of the abbot, for whatever is done without his permission is vainglorious and devoid of merit.[45]

[42] *Benedictine Monachism*, p. 191.

[43] *Commentary on the Rule of Saint Benedict* (New York: Benziger Bros., 1921), 300-301.

[44] "Si animae vero peccati, causa fuerit latens, tantum abbati aut spiritalibus senioribus patefaciant; qui sciant curare et sua et aliena vulnera, non detergere et publicare."—*MPL*, LXVI, 694; *CR*, I, 120.

[45] "Hoc ipsum tamen quod unusquisque offert, abbati suo suggerat et cum eius fiat oratione et voluntate: quia quod sine permissione patris spiritualis fit, praesumptioni deputabitur et vanae gloriae, non mercedi. Ergo cum voluntate abbatis omnia agenda sunt."—*MPL*, LXVI, 756; *CR*, I, 120.

Thus, even supererogatory mortifications are subject to the discretion of the abbot. St. Benedict contends that the only way to avoid illusion in the practice of mortification is by manifesting these good intentions to the superior and to abide by his decision.

St. Benedict incorporates the manifestation of conscience into his monastic legislation, as an implicit instrument of spiritual advancement. The significance of his testimony consists principally in an extension of the area embraced by the manifestation. Under the subject-matter he for the first explicitly includes all tendencies and aspirations towards a more perfect observance. The subsequent history of the manifestation of conscience will evince the extensive influence of the Rule of St. Benedict.

Section 2: *The Regula Magistri* (6th Century)

Among the many Rules which follow that of St. Benedict[46] there is the *Regula Magistri.* The close connection between this lengthy document and the saint's legislation is evident in Chapter Ten which is almost a verbatim reproduction of the above-cited passage on the fifth step of humility:

> Finally the disciple ascends to the fifth degree of humility on the heavenly ladder, if he by humble oral confession does not conceal from the abbot any evil thoughts that enter into the heart nor the evil deeds he has secretly committed.[47]

A later passage of the same Rule represents a further stage of development. In Chapter Fifteen the brethren are exhorted to seek out their spiritual fathers at the first suggestion of serious temptation. On such occasions, the spiritual fathers are urged, on their part, to elicit information from their charges. Thus, the elders are to take the initiative lest the subjects, for reasons of shame and embarrassment, prove reluctant to speak of matters which are of such an intimate nature.[48]

[46] E.g., *Regula Sanctorum Pauli et Stephani, MPL,* LXVI, cols. 949-958; *CR,* I, 138-144. *Regula Incerti Auctoris, MPL,* LXVI, 995-998; *CR,* I, 137-138. *Regula Consensoria Monachorum, MPL,* LXVI, 993-996; *CR,* I, 136-137. *Cujusdam Patris Regula ad Monachos, MPL,* LXVI, cols. 985-994; *CR,* I, 220-224.

[47] "Deinde quintum humilitatis gradum in scala coeli ascendit discipulus, si omnes cogitationes malas cordi suo advenientes, vel mala a se absconse commissa, per humilem linguae confessionem abbati non celaverit suo."—*MPL,* LXXXVIII, col. 969.

[48] "Ergo cum alicui fratri cogitatum malum in corde advenerit, et senserit se exinde fluctuari, statim suis hoc praepositis fateatur, et, mox, oratione facta, nuntiet

Aside from a passing reference in St. Basil and Evagrius Ponticus,[49] this is the first time the initiative is consigned to the superior or spiritual father. Up to this time, as a general rule, the inaugural step of the manifestation rested with the religious subject, for the spiritual master was not to assume a more active role than that of a fatherly recipient. Here the position is reversed. Lest shame or simplicity induce a harmful reticence in their disciples, the spiritual elders are themselves here empowered to make the first effort.

By way of adjunct, the *Regula Tarnatensis,* likewise closely linked with the Rule of St. Benedict, may be considered at this point.[50] Chapter Eight is directed towards the recipients of spiritual confidences. It outlines a threefold obligation: they are not to reject those who come for consolation, they are not to communicate to others the confidences revealed to them, they are to offer appropriate exhortations.[51]

A common factor links the *Regula Magistri* and the *Regula Tarnatensis:* both are predominantly concerned with the role of the spiritual elder in the manifestation of conscience.

Section 3: *Testimony of St. Dorotheus* (6th Century)

St. Dorotheus, founder of a monastery near Gaza about the year 540, was an ascetical writer of note.[52] In a passage of the *Doctrina V*[53] his interest centers on the necessity and advantages of the manifestation for those aspiring after ascetical perfection. He coordinates spiritual progress with the right use of this spiritual practice. In fact, the saint describes the manifestation in terms of an invaluable source of wisdom.

---

hoc ipsum abbati. Nam ipsi praepositi hoc ipsum ultro semper debent a susceptis suis exquirere: ne forte aut res pravas aut turpes fratrem pudeat confiteri. Sed sum ultro ausus magis a majore acceperint, jam fiducialiter sine verecundia indicent cogitata peccata: quod et ipsi praepositi, si et ipsi quod senserit, referant et de se abbati."—*MPL,* LXXXVIII, col. 981.

[49] Cf. *supra,* pp. 4-6; 7-8.

[50] Both Migne and Holstensius-Brockie place this Rule shortly after the time of St. Benedict.—*MPL,* LXVI, cols. 977-986; *CR,* I, 179-186.

[51] "Qui cogitationum impugnationes consolationis suae causa secretius confitetur, non oportet eum despici, nec aliis publicari, sed quantum in se est, blanda exhortatione foveri."—*MPL,* LXVI, col. 980.

[52] "Saint Dorotheus," *Oxford Dictionary,* p. 417.

[53] *MPG,* LXXXVIII, cols. 1675-1686.

Safeguarded against the attacks of the devil, the soul which is open to its spiritual guide experiences the full benefit of moral discipline.[54]

No less a theologian than Suarez considers St. Dorotheus' remarks significant enough to be singled out in his treatise on the Manifestation:

> St. Dorotheus stresses how necessary it is for a man to be guided by another, and that he should not consider himself equal to the task . . . It is necessary for a religious to reveal all hidden realities, in order to be guided and instructed by one wiser than himself.[55]

It is clear, therefore, that St. Dorotheus envisions the manifestation of conscience as an effective means for ascetical progress. In fact, if his words are interpreted literally, the manifestation is a necessary condition for such advancement. Neither director nor directee can achieve their common objective unless the religious opens his heart. The basic import of St. Dorotheus' contribution lies in this emphasis upon the close and necessary relationship between effective spiritual direction and the manifestation of conscience.[56]

Section 4: *Testimony of St. John Climacus* (c. 570-649)

St. John Climacus, an abbot of Sinai, adds a further determination to the concept of the manifestation in his famous *Scala Paradisi*. In *Gradus IV* he advises the monk to carry a small notebook with him and to enter into it whatever passes through his mind in the course of the

[54] "Si enim ipsi cavet anima, ex eo quod omnia occulta sua manifestat, ex eo quod obedit alteri sapientiori qui se instruat, hoc ut faciat, illud ut fugiat, hoc bonum esse, illud item malum, hoc justitam, illud appetitum audit non esse item tempus hujus rei nunc, alias esse tempus; nec invenit diabolus tunc quomodo noceat, quomodo supplantet, cum ex omni parte gubernetur, cum undique tutus sit et cautus."—*MPG*, LXXXVIII, col. 1678.

[55] "Et S. Dorotheus . . . exaggerat quam necessarium sit homini habere a quo regatur, nec sufficientem sibi existimare. Et inde postea concludit, necessarium esse religioso omnia occulta manifestare, ut a sapientiori instrui et regi possit."—*Opera Omnia*, XVI bis, 1084.

[56] Contemporary with the historical period under present discussion are the following Rules: the double Rule of St. Aurelian, Archbishop of Arles from 546-551, namely, the *Regula ad Monachos* (*MPL*, LXVIII, 385-396; *CR*, I, 147-154) and the *Regula ad Virgines* (*MPL*, LXVIII, 397-406; *CR*, I, 368-374); the *Regula ad Monachos* of St. Ferreolus (581) (*MPL*, LXVI, 959-976; *CR*, I, 155-166); and the *Regula S. Leandri Hispalensis Episcopi, sive Liber de Institutione Virginum et Contemptu Mundi, ad Florentinam Sororem*. None of these documents offers any new testimony to the present study.

day. Afterwards the monk is to reveal all these thoughts to his spiritual father[57] in order to receive from him appropriate direction. With this specific detail the manifestation assumes a more ordered form and is proposed as a practice towards which the individual acts of each day are ultimately channeled.

The final testimony from the period under consideration[58] is found in the 9th century *Grimlaici Presbyteri Regula Solitariorum.* The relevant text, in Chapter XXV, is, in large measure, a reiteration of St. Benedict's exhortation concerning the fifth step of humility:[59] "Evil thoughts which enter one's heart are to be brought immediately to Christ. They are to be revealed to one's spiritual elder."[60]

Conclusion

The evidence found within the years 500-1000 is not as extensive as that of the first five centuries. A number of new developments come to light during this second period, however, and add depth and detail to the concept of the manifestation. *St. Benedict,* for example, broadens the scope of the manifestation by including even promptings to a higher life within its ambit. New stress is placed upon the role of the spiritual father who receives the manifestation. The *Regula Magistri* activates this role by empowering him to solicit revelations from his charges, lest the more simple of them refrain from unburdening themselves to him. The *Regula Tarnatensis* lists a number of general norms which the spiritual fathers are to keep before their eyes at all times. *St. Dorotheus* culminates this new emphasis by spelling out the close and necessary relationship between director and directee, and between spiritual direction as such and the manifestation of conscience.

[57]"Illum vero qui triclinio parando erat praefectus hoc factitare curiose observavi. Codicillum gerebat a zona pendentem, in quo quidquid per diem cogitabat, annotate solebat; omnesque cogitationes suas postea Patri, qui coenobio praesidebat, exposuit, quod ex aliis quam plurimis fieri conspexi, et hoc, ut accepi, ex imperio coenobiarchae."—*MPG,* LXXXVIII, col. 702.

[58]The seventh century Rule of St. Isidore of Seville, *S. Isidori Hispalensis Episcopi Regula Monachorum* (*CR,* I, 186-197) offers no testimony of value to the present study.

[59]Cf. *supra,* p. 13.

[60]"Cogitationes malas cordi suo advenientes mox ad Christum allidere. Et seniori spirituali patefacere."—*MPL,* CIII, col. 609.

Finally, it should be noted that throughout the first thousand years, the sole purpose of the manifestation of conscience was the spiritual advancement of the individual religious. There is no explicit awareness of any social benefits which the manifestation might effect or even occasion. How the religious community at large might profit from the manifestation, is the specific feature of later centuries. Treatment of this particular phase of the manifestation falls within the scope of the next chapter.

CHAPTER II

THE FULL DEVELOPMENT OF THE MANIFESTATION OF CONSCIENCE: 1000-1600

At the turn of the millenium, a multiplicity of factors, social, intellectual, political and religious, converge to create an atmosphere in which the religious vocation reaches its apogee as an institutionalized form of life. Monk and hermit, friar and canon, sister and nun are inextricably woven into the ample and complex pattern of the Middle Ages. It is to be expected that this intensity of interest in the religious life should have prompted many re-evaluations of the very nature and function of the same. One phase of this concentrated activity is the founding of many new Orders and the composition of new Rules attempting to exploit the abundant resources of a religious phenomenon so vast and varied. However, for all of the new Orders and Rules[1] which rise to the fore during this period, there is comparatively little development of the concept of the manifestation of conscience—perhaps, because, as a general statement, the Founders of this era were more concerned with the broader issues of the religious life.

During the period in question, namely, from the 11th to the 17th century, whatever notable factors were contributed to the manifestation must be traced directly to the efforts of St. Bonaventure and St. Ignatius. The former introduces a distinctively new and unexpected feature, while the latter enlarges upon and stabilizes this element, in addition to interjecting a number of specifications which will eventually carry the manifestation of conscience to its ultimate stage of development. The present chapter is exclusively dedicated to the unique contributions of these two outstanding religious leaders.

[1]E.g., the *Regulae S. Francisci Assisiatis* (1209-1223), *CR,* III, 21-42. The *Constitutiones Fratrum Sacri ac Regalis Ordinis B. V. Mariae de Mercede Redemptionis Captivorum* (1218), *CR,* III, 433-568. The *Regula Carmelitarum* (1226), *CR,* III, 18-20. The *Constitutiones Canonicorum Regularium S. Augustini, habitus Sancti Antonii Abbatis* (1297), *CR,* V, 119-161. The *Constitutiones et Regulae Fratrum Eremitarum Ordinis S. Hieronymi Congregationis Beati Petri de Pisis* (15th century), *CR,* VI, 88-123. The *Constitutiones et Extravagantes Ordinis Monachorum S.P. Hieronymi Maximi Ecclesiae in Hispania,* (14th century), *CR,* VI, 1-87. The *Constitutiones Congregationis Clericorum Regularium Theatinorum* (1524), *CR,* V, 342-369. None of these Rules, however, yields any new evidence to the present effort.

ARTICLE 1: TESTIMONY OF ST. BONAVENTURE (1221-1274)

Although St. Bonaventure never authored a full scale Rule, he is without question an eminent authority on the religious life, by virtue of his far-reaching religious reforms and his perceptive treatises on many of its aspects. His treatise on the discretion required of superiors furnishes testimony of the highest value on the manifestation of conscience.[2] He states that the proper government of a religious society demands that a superior be on truly intimate terms with each and every member of his community. More specifically, he says that the superior is to have immediate and precise knowledge of the conduct, qualifications, and also consciences of his subjects: *mores et conscientias et vires perspicue agnoscat.*[3]

The Seraphic Doctor compares the provincial and local superiors to Aaron and his sons, remarking that they ought to "go in, that is, they ought to know the internal dispositions of each of the subjects."[4] This intimate knowledge, according to the saint, may be utilized by the superiors to apportion the burdens of religious observance, according to the varying capacities of their subjects.[5]

The most effective means by which superiors can gain a knowledge of "the conduct, qualifications and consciences" of their subjects is through the confidences which the latter share with those in authority. When St. Bonaventure states that such information may appropriately be used in "apportioning the burdens of religious observance," he removes the manifestation of conscience from an interpersonal framework and sets it within the social forum. Up to this time, the sole purpose of the

[2]*Doctoris Seraphici S. Bonaventurae S.R.E. Episcopi Cardinalis Opera Omnia* (10 vols., Ad Aquas Claras: Typographia Collegii S. Bonaventurae, 1882-1902), VIII, 142-147. (Hereafter cited *Opera Omnia.*)

[3]*Opera Omnia,* VIII, 143.

[4]". . . debent intrare, id est, interiora cujusque agnoscere."*Loc. cit.*

[5]"Ad statum debitum tenendum convenit, ut rector omnium subditorum mores et conscientias et vires perspicue agnoscat, ut secundum quod unicuique expedit, onus observantiae regularis imponat. Non enim omnes omnia possunt aequaliter, et, 'unusquisque proprium habet donum ex Deo, aliis, sic, aliis vero sic' (I Cor., 7:7); 'Aaron et filii ejus intrabunt, ipsi quoque disponent onera singulorum . . . quid portare quis debeat' (num. 4:49). Aaron et filii ejus sunt praelati majores et minores, qui debent intrare, id est, interiora cujusque agnoscere, et secundum quod convenit, singulis onus religiosae conversationis imponere et propter triplicem observantiae qualitatem . . ."—*Opera Omnia,* VIII, 143.

manifestation had been the spiritual benefit of the individual religious. Furthermore, the information revealed in confidence had been safeguarded by strict secrecy. Now, however, the superior is at liberty to apply this knowledge for the good of the community at large, as well as for the good of the subject concerned. This is the first recorded testimony in which a social purpose for the manifestation is given recognition. Such an approach constitutes an unprecedented orientation, and ushers in an entirely new stage in the evolution of the manifestation.

There is no doubt that St. Bonaventure desired superiors to employ this confidential knowledge primarily for the spiritual benefit of the subjects themselves. Only in an indirect manner does he refer to the use of this knowledge in the external government of the community.[6] None the less, even this passing reference is of no little consequence, because it provides the nucleus of a practice which St. Ignatius of Loyola eventually developed into an integral part of his legislation. In view of the wide range of activities engaged in by his followers, St. Ignatius will insist that knowledge acquired through the manifestation be used for a more efficient administration of the Society, as well as for the spiritual guidance of the individual Jesuit.[7]

Article 2: Testimony of St. Ignatius of Loyola (1491-1556)

It is only under the aegis of the Jesuits, as already indicated, that the manifestation of conscience comes to full term. For in adopting this by now familiar yet still rather generic implement, and by effecting a number of adjustments, St. Ignatius and the first legislators of the Society of Jesus transformed the manifestation into a rigidly controlled yet rewarding apparatus of the spiritual life.

In the interests of clarity and orderly procedure, the role of St. Ignatius in the development of the manifestation will be considered from a general and then a specific viewpoint, thus:

[6]"Spiritualia vero et quae ad salutem necessaria sunt et profectum virtutum principaliter debet animarum custos et rector sibimet curanda retinere, cum haec sint de substantia officii pastoralis, et de his maxime sit in iudicio rationem Domino redditurus. Haec sunt . . . ad ipsum pertinet conscientias singulorum agnoscere et de quibuslibet perplexitatibus expedire, pericula peccatorum providere et praecavere . . . informare singulos, qualiter officia sibi commissa congrue administrent . . ."—*Opera Omnia,* VIII, 145.

[7]Korth, *The Evolution of "Manifestation of Conscience" in Religious Rules* (Rome: Società Grafica Romana, 1949), p. 93.

Section 1: The manifestation of conscience within the Society;
Section 2: Innovations sponsored by the Jesuits.

This second point is best examined under a threefold division:

A) the manifestation of conscience and the external regimen;
B) the obligation and frequency of the manifestation;
C) the numeric extension of recipients of the manifestation.

Section 1: *The Manifestation of Conscience within the Society*

That the manifestation of conscience held an important place in the mind of St. Ignatius cannot be doubted, much less denied. Already in the formative years of the Society, even before the Constitutions had attained final development, the saint revealed the direction which his interpretation of the religious life would take by presenting his followers with a few basic rules. One historian describes the situation as follows:

> The final matter for which Ignatius had now to provide, that his society might be permanent, was the drawing up of Constitutions. As with Saint Francis of Assisi, this was the last thing attended to, and was preceded by temporary regulations. Necessarily, practice and experience precedes theory, which is to a certain extent based on them. As an interim aid, he distributed among the professed members a set of written rules, nine in number...[8]

Discussions on the precise number and arrangement of these interim prescriptions have been raised, but as these points fall within the province of the historian, it suffices to note them in passing here.[9]

[8]Thompson, *Saint Ignatius of Loyola* (Burns, Oates and Washburne: Manchester, 1909), p. 160.

[9]Thompson, *loc. cit.*, who gives no reference, seems to have taken the *Nine Rules* from Stuart Rose, *Saint Ignatius Loyola and the Early Jesuits* (London, 1891), 295-296. This work of Rose gives this reference: "Bartoli, *Vita di S. Ignazio* 1. iii 1; another version in Cartas t. ii. p. 476." B. Bartoli, *Della Vita e Dell'Istituto di S. Ignatio* [*sic*] *Fondatore della Compagnia di Giesu* [*sic*] *Libri Cinque* (Roma, 1650), 313-315, gives the same rules as Stuart Rose, but to the number of four.

On the other hand, *Cartas de San Ignacio de Loyola Fundador de la Compagnia de Jesu* (Tome II, Madrid, 1875), 476, gives twelve rules and in an order different from Bartoli, Rose, and Thompson. *Monumenta Historica Societatis Jesu* (ed. D. F. Zapico, Romae, 1948), Vol. 71, 141-143, under twelve headings (as in *Cartas*) gives *Avisos de N. Bto. Pe. Ignacio.* The ninth of these reads:

> "No debemus callar las tentaciones, ni sun los pensamientos que paracen buenos; mas debemos los comunicar con nuestros confessores *o superiores,* quia 'Sathanas transfigurat se in angelum lucis,' y todas nuestras cosas devemos hazer por parecer u consejo de nuestro Padres spirituales mas que por nuestro, antes el nuestro siempre le debemos tener pro sospechoso." ("We should not hide our temptations, not even those thoughts which seem to be good; but we should

Be this as it may, it is important to examine the saint's position as reflected in one of these temporary regulations:

> They [the members of the Society] are to see in their Superiors the Image of God Himself, assured that obedience is a guide which cannot be misled. They are *to reveal all their thoughts* as well as actions to those appointed over them, knowing that we must ever mistrust our own judgment.[10]

This direct statement of the founder's will, by reason of its phraseology no less than its historical context, is a compelling indication of how highly St. Ignatius adjudged the values of the manifestation.

Nor does the necessity of opening the heart to the superior undergo a decline of emphasis after the death of St. Ignatius. In fact, No. 33 of the *Regula Provincialis* enjoins upon Provincials the single-minded and diligent observance of the manifestation of conscience, in view of the great importance, both for the glory of God and of the Society, which St. Ignatius assigned to it. This norm also sets down a number of safeguards and reminds the Provincials of the prudence and circumspection necessary for so delicate a matter. By way of positive exhortation, those who receive the manifestation of conscience are to conduct themselves with the kindness that is proper to the head of a family, so that consolation is assured the subject.[11]

A final attestation of the importance attached to the manifestation of conscience by the Society is gleaned from the Decrees of the Fifth General Congregation convoked by Pope Clement VIII, in 1593.[12]

---

manifest them to our confessors *or superiors,* and we must do everything according to the opinion and advice of our spiritual fathers rather than our own, which is to be considered suspicious.") (Emphasis supplied in the original and translation.)

[10]Thompson, *loc. cit.* (emphasis supplied), who cites this as Rule 2, among these temporary regulations.

[11]"Quod in Summaria Constitutionum, p. 40, praescribitur de manifestanda conscientia, id magni momenti ad Dei gloriam et Societatis nostri bonum Pater noster sanctae memoriae Ignatius existimavit: quare ut omni diligentia et animi sinceritate serventur, Provinciali curandum erit. Et cum quisque dixerit quae dicere voluerit iuxta instructionem datam, poterit Provincialis, si qua existimaverit amplius interroganda, id etiam facere; quamvis, quae hominem pudore multum afficerent, ea extra confessionem interroganda non essent. Nec a singulis singula petet, sed prudenter, et circumspecte pro ratione personarum. Denique eam suavitatem teneat, ut illa omnia non tamquam iudex exigere, sed ut benignus parens ob subditi consolationem cognoscere velle videatur."—*Institutiones,* III, 88; *CR,* III, 140-141.

[12]*Institutiones,* II, 262-288.

This assembly declared that the basic features (*substantialia*) of the Institute are to be found in those dispositions in the Pattern of Life or Rule of the Society submitted to Pope Julius III, and confirmed both by him and his successors. The assembly proceeds to enumerate three provisos, indispensable in practice for the fulfillment of these *substantialia*. The last of these reads: "An account of conscience must be rendered to the superior."[13]

Various other arguments might be subjoined to these selections. However, these suffice to establish the immediate point at issue. For these three declarations drawn from the authentic sources of Jesuit legislation provide cogent evidence that St. Ignatius attached to the manifestation of conscience a degree of singular importance.

Section 2: Innovations Sponsored by the Jesuits

Within the framework of the legal system of the Society the manifestation of conscience underwent several modifications. These changes were not concerned with the nature or internal structure of the practice, for this is the merit of the earliest writers on the subject. The specific developments contributed by St. Ignatius dealt with what might be termed certain extrinsic features. These, in brief, are: the relation of the manifestation to the social order in the community; the obligation and frequency of the manifestation; the qualitative circumscription of those who are to receive the manifestation of conscience.

A) The Manifestation of Conscience and the External Regimen

Easily the most fundamental change introduced under Jesuit auspices is the enlargement of the purpose and perspective of the manifestation. In the writings of St. Bonaventure it was suggested that knowledge acquired from such spiritual revelations might conveniently be used in the external government of the community. Under Ignatius the suggestion becomes an accomplished fact. The relative position of both men

[13]"Substantialia Instituti ea in primis sunt, quae in Formula seu regula Societatis, Iulio III, Summo Pontifici proposita, et ab eo aliisque ejus successoribus confirmata, continentur. Deinde ea, sine quibus illa, aut nullo modo, aut vix constare possunt, cuiusmodi sunt:

Primo, esse aliqua impedimenta essentialia in admittendo.

Secundo, non esse necessarium, ut in dimittendo forma iudicalis servetur.

Tertio, reddendam esse Superiori conscientiae rationem."—*Institutiones,* II, 282.

may suggestively be summarized by the verb used in either case: Bonaventure has *convenit* (it is befitting), while the Jesuit legislators, reflecting the mind of their founder, use *refert* (it is advantageous).[14] Congruity has become benefit.

The *Examen Generale,* to exemplify, states that superiors are to have full knowledge of the propensities and movements of the souls of their subjects. This intimate knowledge will enable superiors to fulfill the purposes of the Society and in particular it will help them to avoid placing too burdensome an assignment upon a given religious.[15] No longer is the manifestation of conscience simply a means of fostering the individual's efforts along the way of perfection. While this objective is not lost sight of, a whole series of community advantages is brought into focus. The knowledge derived from the manifestation may now be applied towards a more efficient operation of the corporate membership. As a result of such information, for example, the superiors may decide not to appoint a man to a position which otherwise might have been assigned him. Clearly, such an orientation of the manifestation considerably narrows the margin of miscalculation in the assignment of responsibilities, affords those in authority a more effective control of any eventuality, and, in general, guarantees a high degree of efficiency in the over-all regimen of the Society.

A second reference to such use of this knowledge is found in the same *Examen Generale,* where it is stated:

> Having considered the matter in the Lord, it has appeared to us in the awesome presence of the Divine Majesty, so to arrange matters that subjects are fully known to the superiors, the better to be ruled and governed, as also to be guided by them along the way of the Lord.[16]

[14] Cf. the immediately following footnote with n. 5, *supra,* p. 21.

[15] "Ut melius secundum Dei voluntatem hujusmodi missiones fiant, his et non illis mittendis, vel his ad hoc munus, illis vero ad alia, non solum refert valde, sed summopere, ut Superior plenam habeat notitiam propensionum ac motionum animi, et ad quos defectus vel peccata fuerint vel sint magis propensi et incitati, qui sub ejus cura sunt, ut, ejus rei habita ratione, melius ipsos dirigere possit, nec supra mensuram virium suarum in periculis, vel laboribus gravioribus, quam in Domino ferre suaviter possint, constituat."—*Institutiones,* II, p. 14, n. 35.

[16] "Re in Domino considerata, visum nobis est in divinae majestatis conspectu mirum in modum conferre, ut Superioribus subditi omnino perspecti sint, quo melius regi et gubernari, et per eos in viam Domini dirigi possint."—*Institutiones,* II, p. 14, n. 34.

When this passage is examined in the light of the importance given the manifestation of conscience in the early legislation of the Society, it seems clear that the objectives here envisioned can be attained only by the intimacy and thoroughness of knowledge which comes from the manifestation. The Latin verbs *regi* and *gubernari* certainly indicate real external government and not mere spiritual counsel or direction. Hence the subject's personal revelations to the superior may be employed for the advantage of the Society, over and above the benefits it may afford the individual.

In spite of the dual purpose now in effect, it must be remarked that the spiritual progress of the individual still remained the primary end of the manifestation of conscience.

> ... Saint Ignatius of Loyola sought in this complete manifestation the means of securing a very supernatural and, at the same time, a very paternal government in an order devoted to the most diverse kinds of apostolic work. Was it not of as much importance for the good of the subjects as for that of the faithful that the distribution of employments should be adapted to the moral and spiritual strength and weakness of each one? The candidate for admission was, of course, informed about this conception of religious government. He found in the priestly character and the theological knowledge of his superior sufficient guarantees that his direction would be sound. Besides, the holy founder expressly authorizes the subject to make known in confession only, if he wishes, those faults which are subject matter of sacramental confession. In this case the superior can give to his subordinate the necessary advice, but he must strictly abstain from using these communications in making his decisions about the administrative and disciplinary matters.[17]

Thus, the religious could still derive benefit from the individualized counsel which the superior might offer, without fear that his revelations might prove self-discriminatory in view of the higher interests of the Society as a whole.

B) *The Obligation and Frequency of the Manifestation*

The legislation of the Society expresses in unequivocal terms the obligation of the manifestation of conscience to be made by its members.

> Whoever wishes to follow this Society in the Lord, and to remain herein for the greater glory of God, must manifest his conscience with great humility, purity and charity, under the seal of confes-

[17]Creusen-Ellis, *Religious Men and Women in Church Law* (6 ed., Milwaukee: Bruce, 1957), n. 129, (hereafter cited *Religious Men and Women*).

> sion or of a secret or in any manner that will please him, and this will be for his own greater consolation. He is to keep nothing hidden by which he may have offended the Lord of the Universe; and he should make an integral account of his whole previous life or certainly of things of greater moment to the Superior, who will be one of the Society, or to one of the *praepositi*... And at least every six months he should make this account of himself beginning from the last which he has made. Thus provision is made for the *Coadjutores formati* and the *Professi* to render in the aforesaid manner an account of conscience, to the Superior, once a year, or more frequently if it shall so appear to him.[18]

The obligatory force of the practice is enunciated with such precision that to challenge it is to cavil. While this paragraph applies only to the *Coadjutores formati* and the *Professi,* an ensuing unit in the *Regulae Communes* imposes the obligation upon all others not included in the foregoing categories:

> All [who are not Coadjutors or Professed] must renew their vows twice a year and also make a general confession; and at that time they are also to render an account of their consciences. This is also to be done as often as it seems fitting to the superior, according to the custom of the Society.[19]

Hitherto the use of the manifestation had as a rule been determined by a need on the part of the individual religious. When a problem arose, the subject opened his heart for the sake of direction and consolation. Former religious founders and legislators had encouraged this, but the option of using the manifestation was left with the subject. The manifestation had been essentially a voluntary practice. With the legislation

[18]"Quicumque hanc Societatem in Domino sequi volet, et in eadem ad maiorem Dei gloriam manere, sub sigillo confessionis vel secreti vel quacumque ratione ei placuerit, et ad maiorem ipsius consolationem fuerit, debet conscientiam suam magna cum humilitate, puritate et charitate manifestare, re nulla, qua Dominum Universorum offenderit, celata, et totius anteactae vitae rationem integram vel certe rerum maioris momenti Superiori, qui tum fuerit Societatis, vel cui ex praepositis... et sexto quoque mense rationem hanc sui, ab ultima, quam reddiderit, incipiendo quique reddet. Sic etiam videtur, quod Coadjutores formati et Professi singulis annis, vel crebrius, si Superiori videbitur, suae conscientiae rationem dicto modo ei reddant." —*Institutiones,* III, 8.

[19]"Omnes [qui Professi aut formati Coadjutores non sunt] bis in anno sua vota renovabunt, praemissa confessione generali; quo tempore rationem suae conscientiae reddent, et quoties etiam Superiori visum fuerit, juxta morem Societatis."—*Institutiones,* III, 10.

Part VI of the first chapter of the *Constitutiones* prescribes that the Professi themselves are to make the manifestation once each year (Chapter I, no. 2).

of the Society, however, the manifestation ceases to be facultative. It has become an obligatory practice, binding upon all and calling for fulfillment at stipulated intervals.

C) The Numeric Extension of the Recipients of the Manifestation

One final area of the manifestation is specifically determined by the legal enactments of the Jesuit Order: the designation of those members of the Society who are qualified to receive these confidences of the spiritual life. At the time of St. Benedict only the abbot and a few spiritual seniors were singled out for receiving these revelations. Now, the jurisprudence of the Society imparts this responsibility to all superiors and at times even to their delegates: "They [the subjects] are not to conceal temptation from the prefect of spiritual matters, or from the confessor or from the superior. Indeed, they are to open their entire soul to these..."[20] This numeric extension of qualified recipients is also provided for in No. 23 of the *Regulae Praepositi,*[21] which prescribes that the manifestation be made at stated times to the *Praepositus* or to others deputed by him.[22]

The acknowledged purpose of the manifestation is to aid superiors in the day to day government of the Society. Since it is impossible for the General and Provincial superiors to have the frequent and immediate contacts required for that purpose, the extension of the right to receive the manifestation must of necessity be such as to include lesser superiors who are in daily contact with their subordinates.[23]

[20]"Nullam debent celare tentationem quam Praefecto rerum spiritualium vel confessario, vel superiori non aperiant; imo vero animam suam illis integre manifestam esse, pergratum habeant..."—*Institutiones,* III, 8.

[21]This set of rules is found in *Institutiones,* III, 98-105; *CR,* III, 141-147.

[22]"Efficiat, ut sibi, aut aliis ab ipso deputatis statis temporibus ratio conscientiae reddatur juxta modum, qui in officio Provincialis praescribitur..."—*Institutiones,* III, 99.

[23]Suarez alludes to the opening of the heart to a number of superiors and points out a problem which can result from this. Since it happens that the lesser superiors are frequently changed and that the subjects are also transferred from place to place, the situation can arise where a subject has given an account of conscience to any number of Fathers in the province. This he says can make the manifestation extremely difficult.—*Opera Omnia,* XVI bis, 1082.

Conclusion

Although only two sources of appreciable testimony are found from the 11th to the 17th century, namely, the writings of St. Bonaventure and the early Jesuit legislation, their value and influence are of the greatest moment. *St. Bonaventure* initiates a major transformation of the manifestation by proposing to broaden its scope, in order to encompass the government of the community at large as well as the direction of the individual religious. *St. Ignatius* and the early Jesuits encourage and effect this transformation by giving concrete application to St. Bonaventure's proposal and by inaugurating other modalities. The manifestation is no longer made to higher superiors only, but to many lesser authorities as well. The manifestation loses its facultative status, and becomes a binding practice to be performed at designated times and regulated intervals. These determinations, beyond the unique priority afforded the manifestation by the Society, complete the long and involved process of evolution. Under the legislation of the Society of Jesus, therefore, the manifestation of conscience achieves the full measure of its basic development.

CHAPTER III

COMMON LAW AND THE MANIFESTATION OF CONSCIENCE: (1600 TO THE PRESENT TIME)

The role of the common law in the development of the manifestation has been largely a negative one. Its relation to the subject at hand can be described under two historical divisions of unequal duration.

On the one hand, throughout the first eighteen centuries, the supreme legislator had limited his activity to the approbation of particular religious laws prescribing the manifestation. The attitude of the Church may be summarized in terms of an abstention from direct legislation on the matter—an extended silence, as it were, interrupted by a single, isolated reference. This occurs in the Constitution *Cum ad regularem,* issued by Pope Clement VIII, under the date of March 19, 1603.[1] Although this document does not use the phrase *manifestation of conscience,* it prescribes that "a daily opening of the interior movements of the heart and a manifestation of temptations" be made by novices to their masters. From the beginning of the 17th to the middle of the 19th century, therefore, the manifestation had been the exclusive property of particular religious law and of ascetical writers.[2]

The second historical phase begins with the mid-19th century. At this time the increasing interest of the Church in the manifestation finds successive expression in the regulation, de-emphasis, and ultimate abrogation of the obligatory or elicited manifestation. By a gradual positive process, particular law had in the course of the centuries altered the manifestation from an ascetical aid, optional to the individual, into a legally imposed practice. By a corresponding negative process on the part of the Holy See, from the years 1850-1917, the manifestation re-

[1] *Codicis Iuris Canonici Fontes cura Emi Petri Card. Gasparri editi* (9 vols. Romae [later Civitate Vaticana]: Typis Polyglottis Vaticanis, 1923-1939. Vols. VII-IX ed. *cura et studio Emi Iustiniani Card. Seredi*), n. 189 (hereafter cited *Fontes*).

[2] Excellent ascetical analyses of the manifestation during this period were offered, for example, by Rodriguez (†1616), *Christian Perfection* (3 vols., New York: Kenedy), III, 315-362; Baker, (1575-1614), *Holy Wisdom* (London: Burns and Oates); Schram (1722-1797), *Institutiones Theologiae Mysticae* (Augustae Vindelicorum, Matthaei Rieger P.M. Filiorum, 1777).

verts to its free and spontaneous character, through a gradated series of juridical acts.

The first of these, consisting of a number of particular replies from the Sacred Congregation of Bishops and Regulars, demands that all references to the obligatory or elicited manifestation be expunged from the Constitutions of lay institutes submitted to it for approval. The second expression of the Holy See is represented by the decree *Quemadmodum* of 1890, which, being much broader in purpose, abrogates the obligatory or elicited manifestation in all lay religious communities. The final and most comprehensive enactment is embodied in canon 530 of the Code which proscribes the obligatory and elicited manifestation in all religious institutes, clerical as well as lay. Each of these restrictive enactments will be treated in a separate article.

Article 1: Particular Responses of the Sacred Congregation of Bishops and Regulars

During the 17th, 18th, and 19th centuries the ancient religious Orders (e.g., the Dominicans, Carmelites, Franciscans) resisted the invasion of the forum of conscience by administrative and disciplinary superiors.[3] Many modern institutes, however, following the example of the Society of Jesus, adopted the practice of the manifestation. Side by side with this widespread acceptance there arose a number of abuses, owing mainly to a lack of discretion on the part of superiors.

Doubtless the direction of souls is an exacting art, necessitating great prudence as well as an appreciable knowledge of theology. This direction becomes an especially sensitive matter when the manifestation of conscience is involved, and all the more so when the recipient of such confidential information is also a superior in the external forum. With the diffusion of a practice so delicate, among many lay institutes,[4] it is not difficult to envision concurrent misuses, such as violations of the liberty of conscience and infringement upon the jurisdiction of the confessor. Such was in fact the case, as is evidenced by the words of the Holy See itself:

[3]Langogne, *Manifestation of Conscience* (2 ed., New York; Benziger Brothers, 1892), p. 33.

[4]Wernz-Vidal, *Ius Canonicum ad Codicis Normam exactum* (7 vols. in 8, Romae: apud Aedes Universitatis Gregorianae, 1923-1938), III, n. 212 (hereafter cited *Ius Canonicum*).

> Just as in the fate of human things, how praiseworthy and holy soever they may be in themselves, even so is it with laws wisely enacted, to be liable to be misused and perverted, to purposes opposed and foreign to their nature. Wherefore it sometimes happens that they no longer serve the purposes which the lawmakers had in view: nay, they sometimes even produce quite a contrary result.
>
> Much it is to be deplored that such has proved to be the case with the laws of several Congregations, Societies, and Institutes, both of women who emit simple or solemn vows, and of men who by their profession and discipline are merely laymen. For, inasmuch as occasionally their Constitutions permitted the making of a manifestation of conscience, in order that thereby the members might the more easily learn, in their doubts, from experienced Superiors, how to walk in the path of perfection, it has happened, on the contrary, that some of the latter have introduced the practice of thoroughly inquiring into the state of their subjects' conscience, which is a thing reserved exclusively to the Sacrament of Penance.[5]

During the second half of the 19th century, the Sacred Congregation of Bishops and Regulars became justly concerned and took definite steps to regulate the use of the manifestation of conscience. The Congregation moved slowly and prudently, at first merely deleting all references to this practice in its obligatory and elicited forms from Constitutions of lay institutes submitted to it for approval. The language of the animadversions is strong and clear in every instance. To cite one example: "the manifestation of conscience is restricted to public transgressions of the Rule, and to progress in the virtues, and is to be facultative and not obligatory."[6]

That abuses of different kinds and of varying severity did incite this corrective action on the part of the Holy See, is rather clear. One of these particular decrees expressly indicates such motivation: "Because of abuses which have arisen, the manifestation of conscience is no longer approved by the Holy See and must be expunged from Constitutions."[7]

[5]S.C. Ep. et Reg., decr. "Quemadmodum," 17 dec., 1890.—*Fontes,* n. 2017.

[6]"in praesens manifestatio conscientiae restringitur quoad publicas transgressiones regulae, et ad progressum in virtutibus et quidem non obligatorie sed facultative."—*Analecta Iuris Pontificii,* VI (1861), col. 1052.

Other instances may be found in *Collectanea in usum secretariae Sacrae Congregationis Episcoporum et Regularium,* ed. A. Bizzarri (Romae, 1863), pp. 776, 779, 780, 782, 783, 786, 787, 788, 789, 792, 795.

[7]"Ob abusus, qui irrepserunt, manifestatio conscientiae non amplius ab Apostolica

A third reply emphasized the obvious need for the immediate intervention of the Congregation. This response imposes the deletion of the obligatory and elicited practice of the manifestation from the Constitutions here in question, because it too closely resembled sacramental confession and deserved to be censured as false mysticism.[8]

These particular decrees of the Holy See mark the inception of an attitude which grew more and more stringent, and finally culminated in sweeping legislation abrogating the obligatory and elicited manifestation of conscience.

During these later decades of the 19th century, the Congregation of Bishops and Regulars limited its concern to the Constitutions of new institutes. No steps were taken to remove the obligatory and elicited manifestation from the Constitutions of older Religious communities. This is accomplished in the last decade of the century, by the promulgation of the Decree *Quemadmodum,* in 1890,[9] the second step in the Holy See's studied effort against the abuses connected with the manifestation of conscience.

Article 2: The Decree "Quemadmodum" (1890)

This decree is a supreme effort on the part of the Holy See to remove the abuses which had arisen in some lay institutes as a result of the indiscretions of superiors and superioresses. When viewed in the light of anterior particular responses concerning the manifestation of conscience, the decree can hardly be pronounced an unexpected innovation, or a hasty intrusion upon right and justice. Thus, there is no question here of a law new in all its bearings, but only of certain dispositions against and new restrictions of abuses, in order to restore to usefulness an effective practice distorted by corrupting influences. Hence, *Quemad-*

Sede probatur. Idcirco a constitutionibus expungenda erit."—*Analecta Iuris Pontificii,* IX (1867), col. 272.

[8]"En 1854 la S. Congregation examinait les constitutions d'un institut de religieuses recemment fonde, Le Rme consulteur proposa plusieurs corrections, qui furent agreees par les Emes Cardinaux, Or, sur l'article de la direction, et par rapport au compte de conscience, le consulteur fit les observations suivantes . . .

'Je ne puis pas approuver,' disait le Rme consulteur, 'ce compte-rendu detaille secret. Cela ressemble trop a la confession sacramentelle, et, pourrait etre consure comme un faux mysticisme.' "—*Analecta Juris Pontificii,* IV (1860), col. 1325.

[9]S. C. Ep. et Reg., decr., 17 dec., nos. 1, 2, 7.—*Fontes,* n. 2017.

modum represents the terminal development of the many previous statements issued by the Congregation of Bishops and Regulars.

The decree is concerned with eradicating incorrect procedures regarding three kindred areas of the religious life: the manifestation of conscience, the recourse to extraordinary confessors, and the frequency of Communion.

Its first precept steers clear of equivocation, ambiguity, and compromise, by striking immediately at the roots of the obligatory and elicited manifestation:

> His Holiness annuls, abrogates, and declares of no force whatever, hereafter, all regulations whatsoever in the Constitutions of Pious Societies and Institutes of women who emit either simple or solemn vows, as well as in those of men of the purely lay order (even though the said constitutions should have received from the Holy See approbation in any form soever, even that which is termed most special), in this one point, in which these Constitutions regard the secret manifestation of conscience in whatsoever manner or what name soever. He therefore enjoins on all Superiors, Male and Female, of such Institutes, Congregations, and Societies, to absolutely cancel and expunge altogether from their respective Constitutions, Directories, and Manuals, all the aforesaid regulations. Likewise, he declares whatsoever usages and customs in this matter, even such as are from time out of mind, to be null and void and to be abolished.[10]

The juridical effect of this pontifical enactment is the unqualified abrogation of all legislation commanding the manifestation of conscience in lay institutes, the effect of custom, even immemorial, to the contrary notwithstanding. This initial ruling sets forth the import and scope of the decree by designating the subjects who are encompassed, namely, all religious women and all lay religious men who are members of purely lay communities, e.g., the Brothers of the Christian Schools.[11]

[10]*Fontes,* n. 2017.—The translation of the decree here used is taken from Sabetti, *The Decree "Quemadmodum," with Explanations* (Baltimore: John Murphy & Co., 1892), who designates it as "... the official translation sent by our Ordinaries to the superiors of those religious communities that are concerned with it." The complete text of this translation is appended to the present work. Cf. *infra,* pp. 91-93.

[11]The following doubt was proposed to the Congregation of Bishops and Regulars: "Whether the Decree comprised, besides the institutes of women, only those institutes of men of purely lay character, as the Brothers of the Christian Schools, etc., or embraces also ecclesiastical congregations like the Salesians, founded by Don Bosco, the Rosminians, Lazarists, and the like, in which besides priests, many lay brothers are numbered?"

Lest this first ruling be stripped of its efficacy and fall short of its intended purpose, it is supplemented by a second which details the new obligations of superiors in this matter.

> He [His Holiness], moreover, forbids absolutely such Superiors, male and female, no matter what may be their rank and eminence, from endeavoring, directly or indirectly, by command, counsel, fear, threats, or blandishments, to induce their subjects to make to them any such manifestation of conscience; and he commands these subjects on their part to denounce the higher Superiors such as dare to induce them to make such manifestation; and if the guilty one be the Superior-General, the denunciation should be made by them to this Sacred Congregation.[12]

The possibility is foreseen that some superiors, while respecting the prohibition to command the manifestation, might nevertheless draw their subjects, by means of flattery, counsel, or exhortation, to a full manifestation of their interior life. Against such evasiveness there is formulated this second norm which imposes a double prescription: one absolute, prohibiting superiors to have recourse to threats, commands, counsels and the like; the other conditional, directing that superiors who are guilty of such conduct be denounced to the proper authority.

Having shorn the manifestation of its obligatory character, *Quemadmodum* proceeds to ratify the practice in its free and spontaneous form.

> This ... in nowise hinders subjects from freely and of their own accord opening their hearts to their Superiors, for the purpose of obtaining from their prudence, counsel and direction, in doubts and perplexities, in order to aid them in acquiring virtues and advancing in perfection.[13]

As the Holy See was concerned only with abrogating the obligatory and elicited manifestation, subjects are still at liberty to lay open the state of their souls to superiors and to draw advantage from their knowledge and experience, for their own consolation and direction.

In the closing section of the decree the legislator emphasizes the urgency of the matters at issue by surrounding their violation with automatically incurred sanctions, and by ordering that the contents of the

---

The Congregation, on April 15th, 1891, answered *affirmatively* to the first part, *negatively* to the second.—*Acta Sanctae Sedis* (41 vols., Romae: Ex Typographia Polyglotta, 1865-1908), XXIV (1891-1892), 190-191.

[12] *Fontes*, n. 2017; Sabetti, *The Decree*, p. 13.

[13] *Fontes*, n. 2017; Sabetti, *The Decree*, p. 14.

decree be brought, at regular intervals, to the attention of all concerned:

> His Holiness, furthermore, commands all Superiors General, Provincials and local Superiors of the Institutes aforementioned, whether of men or women, to observe zealously and accurately the regulations prescribed in this Decree, under pain of incurring ipso facto the penalties decreed against Superiors who violate the mandates of the Holy See.
>
> He lastly commands that copies of this present Decree, translated into the vernacular, shall be inserted in the Constitutions of the said pious Institutes, and that at least once in a twelvemonth, at a stated time in each House, either in the public Refectory, or in Chapter assembled for this special purpose, this Decree shall be read in a loud and intelligible voice.[14]

These final ordinances attempt to guarantee the future inviolable observance of the decree, and to render ineffectual pleas of innocence based on ignorance or desuetude.

In conclusion, it must be noted that *Quemadmodum* makes no reference whatever to clerical religious institutes. As a result, their legislation on this point continued in full force. It is only with the promulgation of the Code of Canon Law that the Church finally effected the universal proscription against the obligatory and elicited manifestation of conscience. It is the function of Canon 530 to extend this proscription to clerical religious institutes as well.

Article 3: Canon 530 and Related Jurisprudence

Canon 530 repeats the prohibition of *Quemadmodum* and forbids the obligatory and elicited manifestation of conscience in language which is more succinct but no less severe:

> §1. All religious superiors are strictly forbidden to induce their subjects by any means whatever to manifest their conscience to them.
>
> §2. Subjects however are not forbidden to open their hearts freely and voluntarily to their superiors; indeed, it is expedient that they should approach their superiors with filial confidence, and, if the superiors are priests, reveal to them the doubts and perplexities of their conscience.

The new law is at once an extension and a restriction of the earlier law. It is an extension, because the prohibition contained in canon 530, §1, is directed not only to superiors of lay religious institutes, but also to superiors of all religious societies, clerical as well as lay. When the

[14] *Fontes*, n. 2017; Sabetti, *The Decree*, pp. 21-22.

decree was promulgated, it appeared that the abuses connected with the manifestation were limited to lay religious institutes for the decree affected these groups alone. Apparently this was a miscontention, for less than thirty years later the Code extended the prohibition to all religious communities without exception. It is a restriction, because canon 530 deletes some dispositions of the decree: e.g., the denunciation of superiors who violate the law, and the censures attached to these violations.

Like *Quemadmodum,* and in strikingly similar language, Canon 530, §2, permits and even encourages subjects to open their hearts to superiors with filial confidence in time of doubt and anxiety.[15]

Since the promulgation of the Code, canon 530 has not been modified. This is verified in each of the six documents referring to the manifestation which have been issued by the Holy See since 1918. For the most part these documents simply allude to or re-state the prohibition voiced by the canon. Because of their contemporary interest, and in order to complete the present historical survey, these documents are here cited in chronological order. No commentary on these post-Code statements of the Holy See is here offered, because this will be adequately provided for by the final two chapters of the present work, which are both dedicated to a commentary on canon 530 itself.[16]

> 1) *March* 25, 1922. Question 68 of the Questionnaire for the Quinquennial Report published by the Sacred Congregation of Religious simply inquires: "Are the canonical statutes being observed: a) insofar as they prohibit the manifestation of conscience?"[17]

[15]A detailed comparison of *Quemadmodum* and canon 530 will be offered in the next chapter, in which it will be shown how the Code law agrees with, extends, and restricts the earlier law. Cf. *infra,* pp. 43-46.

[16]Cf. *infra,* pp. 55-88.

[17]"Num serventur canonica statuta: a) quantum ad conscientiae manifestationem non exigendam."—*Acta Apostolicae Sedis, Commentarium Officiale* (Romae, Typis Polyglottis Vaticanis, 1909-), XIV (1922), 282 (hereafter cited *AAS*).

On June 29, 1923, Pius XI in his holographic decree stated: "Quae Sanctus Ignatius de Loyola in Constitutionibus Soc. Jesu, toties ab antecessoribus Nostris probatis et confirmatis de ratione conscientiae reddenda statuit, suprema Nostra Apostolica Auctoritate iterum probamus et confirmamus... Pius Papa XI."—*Commentarium Pro Religiosis: Publicatio Mensilis Opera et Studio Missioniorum Filiorum Immaculati Cordis Beatae Mariae Virginis* (Romae: 1920-), XII (1931), p. 130, n. 433 (hereafter cited *CpR*).

2) *July* 16, 1931. No. 79 of the Statutes for Extern Sisters, published by the Congregation of Religious, is merely a paraphrase of canon 530: "All religious superiors and superioresses are strictly forbidden to induce their subjects by any means whatever to manifest their conscience to them. Subjects on their part, however, are not forbidden to open their souls freely and spontaneously to their superiors or superioresses."[18] This norm, of course, adapted the canon to the religious in question and therefore deleted the sections which refer only to priest superiors.

3) *June* 29, 1940. The Sacred Congregation of the Propagation of the Faith published an important set of Norms to be applied to the Constitutions of diocesan congregations under its care. No. 81 repeats canon 530, and also interprets it by an explicit extension of the prohibition to mistresses of novices: "All superioresses and mistresses of novices are strictly forbidden to induce in any manner sisters subject to them to make a manifestation of conscience to them. The religious subjects however are not forbidden to open their soul freely and spontaneously to their superiors."[19]

4) *December* 9, 1948. The Sacred Congregation of Religious published a new Questionnaire for the Quinquennial Report of religious. No. 82 of the formula for institutes of pontifical law refers expressly to canon 530, inquiring: "Do superiors, according to the norm of law (c. 530, §§1, 2), leave their subjects free from constraint as regards the making of the manifestation of conscience properly so-called to them?"[20]

5) *February* 9, 1952. The Supreme Pontiff promulgated the new Religious Law for the Oriental Church. Canon 62 simply restates canon 530 of the Latin Code, except that the new canon reads,

[18]"Omnes religiosi superiores et superiorissae districte vetantur personae sibi subditas quoquo modo inducere ad conscientiae manifestationem sibi peragendam. Non tamen prohibentur subditae quominus libere ac ultro aperire animum suum superioribus vel antistitis valeant."—*CpR,* XII (1931), 419.

[19]"Superiorissae omnes et magistrae novitiarum districte vetantur sorores sibi subditas quoquo modo inducere ad conscientiae manifestationem sibi peragendam. Non tamen prohibentur subditae religiosae quominus libere ac ultro animum suum aperiant superioribus."—*Normae pro constitutionibus Congregationum Juris dioecescani a S.C. de Propaganda Fide dependentium* (Romae: Typis Polyglottis Vaticanis, 1940), p. 18 (hereafter cited *Normae of* 1940).

[20]"Utrum superiores liberam, ad normam iuris (c. 530, §§ 1, 2) conscientiae manifestationem proprie dictam sibi faciendam, relinquant."—*Elenchus quaestionum quibus a Religionibus et Societatibus in Relatione ad S. Sedem quinto quoque anno transmittenda respondendum est ad normam Decreti "Cum transactis"* (Romae: Typis Polyglottis Vaticanis, 1949).

"Superiors are severely forbidden," where canon 530 has "superiors are strictly forbidden."[21]

6) *May* 31, 1956. The Apostolic Constitution *Sedes Sapientiae* paraphrases §2 of canon 530: "... the Church desires most eagerly that they [novices and clerical students] open their soul confidently not only to superiors properly so-called according to the norms of law (canon 530, §1) and of the constitutions, but more especially to their Spiritual Masters and Prefects; ... Moreover it is fitting that according to the mind of the law (canon 530, §2), they go to them with filial confidence, revealing to them freely and spontaneously their doubts and anxieties of conscience."[22]

Throughout the decades following the promulgation of the Code, the mind of the Church has not changed concerning the manifestation of conscience. By timely documents, the well-founded and prudent position taken on the subject by *Quemadmodum* and canon 530 has been ratified: the manifestation remains strictly outlawed in its obligatory or elicited form; in its free and spontaneous form, on the other hand, the manifestation continues to be permitted and encouraged.

Conclusion

From the years 1600-1850, aside from a single exception, the Church continued the attitude assumed from the very beginning, as regards the

[21]"§1. Omnes religiosi superiores severe vetantur personas sibi subditas quoquo modo inducere ad conscientiae manifestationem sibi peragendam.

"§2. Non tamen prohibentur subditi quominus libere et ultro aperire animum suum Superioribus valeant; imo expedit ut ipsi filiali cum fiducia Superiores adeant, iis, si sint sacerdotes, dubia quoque et anxietates suae conscientiae exponentes."—*Motu Proprio, de Religiosis ... pro Ecclesiis Orientalibus* (Romae: Typis Polyglottis Vaticanis, 1952).

[22]*The Apostolic Constitution "Sedes Sapientiae and the General Statutes" Annexed to It on the Religious, Clerical, and Apostolic Training to be Imparted to Clerics in the States of Perfection to be Acquired* (Sole Official English Text, Washington, D.C.: The Catholic University of America Press, 1957) p. 40.

It does not seem that this Constitution affords an authentic interpretation of the disputed point as to whether the prohibition of canon 530 affects only superiors properly so-called or also includes officials, such as masters of novices and prefects of students. In its first parenthetical citation of the Code—(canon 530, §1)—the Constitution merely indicates the obvious, namely, the canon cited binds "superiors properly so-called." There is no basis for inferring that this parenthetical reference intends to offer an exhaustive enumeration of those bound by the canon, and thereby to exempt masters of novices and prefects of students. This disputed point is considered in detail in a later chapter. Cf. *infra*, pp. 57-71.

manifestation of conscience. Her position may be identified as one of complete tolerance, in that her juridical activity on this point never reached beyond simple approval of particular laws prescribing the manifestation. With the mid-1800's, however, this centuries-old policy of non-interference was suddenly put aside. Awareness of the increasing inconveniences and the disastrous consequences which might easily ensue upon her tolerant attitude caused her to adopt a direct and decisive course of action.

Her initial efforts took the form of particular responses which eradicated the abuses from the Constitutions of new Institutes. By the closing decade of the last century, her corrective action had intensified to the extent of abrogating the obligatory and elicited manifestation of conscience in all lay or non-clerical institutes. Finally, the full expression of her restrictive legislation found its way into the Code of Canon Law, which abrogates the obligatory and elicited manifestation in all religious institutes, clerical as well as lay. In a word, Canon 530, for all of its unassuming brevity, climaxes seventeen centuries of history relating to the manifestation of conscience.

CANONICAL COMMENTARY

The canonical part of the present work offers a comprehensive treatment of the actual legal status of the manifestation of conscience in the light of canon 530. Chapter IV takes into account a number of important preliminaries by a juxtaposition of the pre-Code law, *Quemadmodum,* with the current legislation in force, and by an inquiry into the juridical signification of the expression, *manifestation of conscience.* In this way the precise nature of the prohibition and recommendation incorporated in canon 530 will be more readily understood.

These general pre-notes provide a foundation for the extended canonical commentary offered in Chapters V and VI, in which the two paragraphs of canon 530 will be given separate treatment.

CHAPTER IV

CANONICAL PRELIMINARIES

ARTICLE 1: RELATIONSHIP OF THE OLD LAW AND THE NEW LAW

As seen in the preceding chapter, canon 530 is an ulterior stage and climax of the decree *Quemadmodum*. This decree is, in fact, cited by Cardinal Gasparri as the sole source of the canon in question.[1] A knowledge of the relationship between the two legislations is essential to a full understanding of canon 530. Accordingly, one section of the present article is devoted to a detailed comparison of the two legislations, while the present interpretative force of *Quemadmodum* will be considered under a distinct section.

Section 1: *Comparison of Quemadmodum and canon* 530

A comparative analysis of these laws lends itself to a twofold division: the first will consider the elements of *Quemadmodum* not incorporated in the Code, the second will treat of the dispositions of the decree embodied in canon 530.

A) Norms of Quemadmodum not contained in the Code

A cursory examination of the text of the decree reveals only one norm which is in opposition to the Code:

> He [His Holiness] ... commands that at least once in a twelvemonth, at a stated time in each House, either in public Refectory, or in Chapter assembled for this special purpose, this Decree shall be read in a loud and intelligible voice.[2]

Canon 509, §2, n. 1, on the other hand states: "At least once a year the local superiors shall have read publicly ... the decrees prescribed to be read by the Holy See." These two dispositions are diametrically opposed: whereas *Quemadmodum* imposed the formal reading of a pre-Code document, canon 509 enjoins the reading of only specified future

[1] Cf. the footnote to canon 530.

[2] *Fontes*, n. 2017; Sabetti, *The Decree*, p. 22.

decrees.[3] Therefore, according to canon 6, nos. 1 & 6, this prescription of *Quemadmodum* is abrogated.

The majority of the norms of *Quemadmodum* are not opposed to the Code, but have simply been omitted by it. Such is the case of: 1) the command to abrogate and suppress all mention of the manifestation of conscience in the particular legislation, both written and customary, of lay religious institutes;[4] 2) the obligation imposed on subjects to denounce superiors who would dare elicit the manifestation of conscience from them;[5] 3) the penalties to be incurred automatically by superiors who transgress the norms of the decree;[6] 4) the command to incorporate the decree into the religious constitutions.[7] These norms of the decree are not opposed to the new law, but since the Code makes no explicit or implicit mention of them, they must be considered as without any juridic force. The ecclesiastical penalties which were incurred automatically (*ipso facto*) by the transgressors of the decree have been abrogated by canon 6, no. 5: "Concerning penalties not mentioned in the Code, whether spiritual or temporal, medicinal or those called vindictive, whether automatically incurred on the commission of an act or imposed by judicial sentence, they are to be considered abrogated." Similarly, all the disciplinary norms not reproduced in the Code lose their force by reason of canon 6, no. 6: "If among the other disciplinary laws hitherto in force, there is one which is neither explicitly or implicitly contained in the Code, it must be said to have lost all force, unless it is found in approved liturgical books or is an ordinance of divine law, positive or natural." Thus there is no further juridical obligation for subjects to denounce superiors, although a moral obligation to do so may arise from other sources. Thus also the obligation to insert the decree into the constitutions has been abrogated.

B) Norms of Quemadmodum contained in the Code

The basic norms of the decree concerning the manifestation are re-

[3]Cf. Michiels, *Normae Generales Juris Canonici* (2 ed., 2 vols., Parisiis, Tornaci-Romae, 1949), I, 122; 656.

[4]*Fontes*, n. 2017; Sabetti, *The Decree*, p. 11.

[5]*Fontes*, n. 2017; Sabetti, *The Decree*, p. 13.

[6]*Fontes*, n. 2017; Sabetti, *The Decree*, p. 21.

[7]*Fontes*, n. 2017; Sabetti, *The Decree*, p. 22.

produced in canon 530. The mutual relationship can be clearly seen from this arrangement in parallel columns:

Quemadmodum	*Canon* 530
He [His Holiness] . . . forbids absolutely such Superiors, male and female, no matter what may be their rank and eminence, from endeavoring, directly or indirectly, by command, counsel, fear, threats, or blandishments, to induce their subjects to make to them any manifestation of conscience...	§1. All religious superiors are strictly forbidden to induce their subjects by any means whatever to manifest their conscience to them.
This, however, in nowise hinders subjects from freely and of their own accord opening their hearts to their Superiors, for the purpose of obtaining from their prudence, counsel and direction, in doubts and perplexities, in order to aid them in acquiring virtues and advancing in perfection.	§2. Subjects however are not forbidden to open their hearts freely and voluntarily to their Superiors; indeed, it is expedient that they should approach their superiors with filial confidence, and, if the superiors are priests, reveal to them the doubts and perplexities of their conscience.

As indicated by the comparative table, canon 530 re-states the norms of the decree, but with two important modifications: it extends the prohibition of eliciting or commanding the manifestation to superiors of all religious institutes, clerical as well as lay,[8] and it adds a special recommendation of the free and spontaneous manifestation of doubts and anxieties of conscience in cases where superiors are priests.

The norms of the decree which are contained at least equivalently in canon 530 would seem, according to canon 6, no. 6, to remain in force. However, it is more exact to specify that these laws are inserted only materially into the Code and not formally, and hence all the juridic force of the law in vigor derives solely from the will of the legislator of the Code, and not at all from the promulgation of the old decree.[9] This is evidenced by canon 22, which states that a later law abrogates an earlier one if it entirely revises the subject matter of the former law.

[8]The Code extends this prohibition to superiors of societies of both men and women living in common without vows. Cf. canon 675.

[9]Vermeersch-Creusen, *Epitome Iuris Canonici* (7 ed., 3 vols., Mechliniae-Romae: H. Dessain, 1949-1956), I, 77, n. 76 (hereafter cited *Epitome*).

Needless to say, the two extensions introduced by canon 530 derive their binding force solely from the Code. Thus none of the norms of the decree *Quemadmodum* as such concerning the manifestation of conscience retains any juridic force.

Section 2: Interpretative Force of "Quemadmodum"

Although the abrogation of *Quemadmodum* by the Code strips it of all juridic force, it retains great value as an interpretative source. Nos. 2, 3, 4, of canon 6, by way of general principles, establish that the interpretative force of an old law depends on whether the text of the Code reproduces the former legislation in a complete or partial manner. The concrete application of these principles to the case at hand makes it quite evident that *Quemadmodum* must serve as a historical and canonical framework for canon 530. In particular, those sections of the decree prohibiting the solicited manifestation in any manner and recommending filial confidence are to be employed as immediate and necessary sources for the proper interpretation of both paragraphs of canon 530. Moreover, those parts of the decree which are not reproduced by the canon, but which are not in opposition thereto, also serve as context for the integral interpretation of the law now in force.

Only those parts of the canon, therefore, which add to the old law, namely, "all" in paragraph 1 which extends the new law to clerical religious, and "indeed it is expedient . . . if they are priests" which introduces the distinction between lay and clerical superiors, must be interpreted according to their own wording.[10] Hence, the full significance of *Quemadmodum* lies in the fact that it supplies materials for the synthesis represented by canon 530. On this fact rests the actual interpretative force of *Quemadmodum*.

Article 2: The Concept of the Manifestation of Conscience

The commentary on canon 530 should be prefaced by a final pre-note: viz., an analysis of the precise nature of the manifestation of conscience. This question will be approached from a twofold angle. Negatively, the manifestation will be compared with a number of similar practices in order to show the points of divergence. Positively, several standard definitions of the manifestation will be examined, after which a number

[10] Cf. canon 6, n. 3.

of divisions will be formulated in order to understand the precise meaning of the manifestation in a strict canonical context.

Section 1: *Comparison of the Manifestation of Conscience with Similar Practices*

A) Sacramental Confession

It is evident that the manifestation of conscience and sacramental confession may be combined in a single act. In such a case, the priest who receives the revelations assumes the twofold role of confessor and director. However, since canon 530 speaks of superiors, and since superiors are expressly forbidden by other laws[11] of the Code to induce their subjects to confess to them, it is clear that the present canon must refer to an extra-sacramental manifestation. This is confirmed by the fact that the prohibition of canon 530 also applies to non-clerical superiors.

There are many differences between confession and the manifestation. The one is a divinely instituted rite, the other a spontaneous ascetical practice. To violate the obligation of secrecy attached to confession is a sacrilege, whereas a similar violation of the manifestation, while sinful, is devoid of the double malice. The basic difference between the manifestation and sacramental confession, however, is one of motivation. The primary motive of confession is absolution; the primary motive of the manifestation of conscience, on the other hand, is direction. This last difference is verified in every case, for even though direction might also be received in sacramental confession, it will always be subordinated to the absolution itself.[12]

There can, of course, also be a difference regarding subject matter.[13] Confession always demands that sin in some form be presented for absolution. The manifestation by no means requires the revelation of sin. However, this does not exclude sin as matter for a given manifestation. Indeed, it seems that a person freely seeking guidance from another will at times have to reveal genuine confessional matter, in

[11]Canons 891 and 518, §§2 & 3.

[12]Cf. Ziegler, *The Obligation of the Confessor to Instruct Penitents*, The Catholic University of America Studies in Sacred Theology, Second Series, No. 121, (Washington, D.C.: Catholic University of America Press, 1959).

[13]Wernz-Vidal, *Ius Canonicum*, III, 167.

order to receive the proper direction. Thus, for example, if a subject freely reveals that he is greatly troubled by temptations against a given virtue, proper and precise direction would seem to demand that he also reveal whether or not he consents to these temptations, and if so, with how much regularity and intensity. This would constitute a manifestation of conscience clearly involving confessional matter, yet fully distinct from confession by reason of the motive for the revelation.

On the surface it might appear that the matter of sacramental confession will always involve a most detailed and penetrating revelation of soul. But this is not necessarily so. A person motivated by a simple and sincere desire for absolution, can make a valid, licit, and fruitful confession in terms which are perfectly clear to the confessor but are none the less technical and undetailed. The same person, on the other hand, making a spontaneous manifestation of conscience on the same matter, but for the purpose of direction, may—often must—go into far more detail if the objective envisioned is to be effectively fulfilled. Thus it is mainly manner and motive, rather than subject matter, which differentiate the manifestation of conscience from sacramental confession.

B) The Chapter of Faults

The manifestation is clearly distinct from the *culpa* or chapter of faults common to many communities. In the first place, the proper matter of the *culpa* are external infractions of community discipline. The material or external aspect of an act, e.g., the slamming of a door, the damaging of community property, is all that should be revealed, never the internal dispositions which may have accompanied the act.[14] The manifestation, on the other hand, embraces far more intimate matters, such as vices, virtues, temptations, and special graces. Secondly, the *culpa* and the manifestation differ as to end. The purpose of the *culpa*, especially when made in public, is mainly to acquire and develop the virtue of humility. The purpose of the intimate manifestation, on the other hand, is direction and guidance in the spiritual life.

C) Paternal Inquiry

The manifestation of conscience also differs from the mere paternal inquiry or *colloquium* practiced in some religious communities.[15]

[14] Vermeersch-Creusen, *Epitome*, I, n. 650.

[15] Some institutes label this: colloquy, personal interview, private conference.

This practice is directed towards the individual good of the subject and may cover such areas as physical needs, academic problems, questions relating to external observance. These examples suggest the basic difference from the manifestation, for the material object is only external matters, not a complete manifestation of the intimate conscience.[16]

The mutual comparisons between the manifestation of conscience and several related yet dissimilar practices clearly set forth what the manifestation is not. A positive approach to the manifestation is now indicated.

Section 2: Positive Concept of the Manifestation of Conscience

A proper understanding of canon 530, it may safely be affirmed, hinges upon an accurate knowledge of what the lawmaker intended by the expression, *manifestation of conscience*. Admittedly this is a broad term, whose accurate meaning is far from being self-explanatory. Here it is expedient to survey a number of definitions, prior to the establishment of various divisions calculated at circumscribing so evasive a phrase as *manifestation of conscience*.

A) Definitions

The classical description of the manifestation was formulated by Suarez, long before the common law addressed itself to the subject. His definition reads: "A manifestation of the state of conscience, made by a subject to his superior, in order to be intimately known by the latter, both in his conduct and in his affections or inclinations."[17] The subject matter of this definition is extremely ample: "the state of conscience." The recipient of the manifestation, on the other hand, is rather limited: "to his superior." The object of this manifestation is the intimate knowledge of the subject by the superior for the purpose of offering appropriate spiritual direction.

Franco, a leading commentator on the decree *Quemadmodum*, writing shortly after its promulgation, proffers this definition:

> ...by manifestation of conscience as it is commonly understood in religious communities, is meant the knowledge of the state of soul, imparted by a subject to a superior, not indeed freely or voluntarily, but because the rule requires it, and so given that the

[16] Wernz-Vidal, *Ius Canonicum*, III, 167.

[17] *Opera Omnia*, XVI bis, n. 2.

dispositions and desires for the performance of good, the obstacles and difficulties encountered, the passions and temptations which move or harass the soul, the faults that are more frequently committed, are sincerely and unreservedly revealed.[18]

This definition specified at great length the areas of spiritual endeavor over which the manifestation may range. The degree of intimacy these spiritual commitments may attain is attested by the phrase, "the passions and temptations which harass the soul." The element of compulsion or imperativeness introduced into the definition may be motivated by the author's intention to explain the historical antecedents of *Quemadmodum*.

Schaefer, writing after the codification of Church Law, interprets the manifestation as a disclosure of the state of the soul made extrasacramentally, concerning matters relating to virtues and vices.[19] He goes on to extend this disclosure to the usual pattern of conduct, affections, inclinations, propensities, temptations, and weaknesses.[20] Here again the subject matter of the manifestation is specifically categorized. In view of the law prohibiting the obligatory and elicited manifestation, the definition purposely forgoes specific mention of those to whom the manifestation may be made.

Creusen-Ellis state that "to manifest one's conscience means to reveal one's hidden faults (with their degree of culpability), one's interior or hidden acts of virtue, one's intentions, the affections and repugnances to which one has yielded, the temptations and trials which God sends, the lights and good desires received from Him."[21] Here again the subject matter of the manifestation is given specific treatment—in point of fact, it constitutes the greater portion of the definition.

Each of these definitions ascribes to the manifestation an extremely broad material object. While Suarez does not descend to particularized enumeration, his attempt at definition is couched in such generic terms that his two categories are effectively co-extensive with the areas described in detail by Schaefer, Franco, and Creusen-Ellis. None of these

[18] *Ad Una Superiora Religiosa Intorno ad un Recente Decreto Pontificio* (2 ed., Modena, 1891). (Hereafter cited *Ad Una Superiora*).

[19] *De Religiosis ad Normam Codis Iuris Canonici* (4 ed., Romae: Typis Polyglottis Vaticanis, 1947), n. 684 (hereafter cited *De Religiosis*).

[20] *Loc. cit.*

[21] *Religious Men and Women*, n. 128.

definitions, it may be remarked, makes any effort at limitation. As a matter of fact, some of the terms employed, e.g., affections, inclinations, propensities, are rather fluid, and it is questionable whether the nebulous concepts which they conjure up make the definitions in which they occur reliable or serviceable. Be this as it may, synthetically, the manifestation is a revelation of the state of conscience to one competent in spiritual matters for the purpose of guidance. There can be no doubt that this revelation must be more specific than that minimally required by the sacrament of penance. It is also clear that the recipient of these spiritual disclosures must be skilled in ascetico-mystical theology, though not necessarily more advanced in spiritual attainments than the one consulting him. It is clear finally that the consultation is regarded by both interested parties as an instrument of spiritual progress. What is not clear is the accurate determination of the phrase, "the state of conscience."

The basic problem, therefore, in attempting to grasp exactly what the legislator means by *manifestation of conscience* revolves around the question of delimiting the material object of the practice in point. A division of the manifestation of conscience according to the various kinds of matter it can embrace, will, it is believed, contribute to a clarification of this problem.

B) *Divisions of the Manifestation*

It is the unconfined character of the material object of the manifestation which renders obscure and tenuous its exact legal signification and proscription. Only by pertinent divisions which delimit this material object can the concept of the manifestation be brought sufficiently under control and the full import and extent of the legislator's prohibition be determined. The ensuing threefold division of the manifestation, therefore, is ultimately motivated by the intention of understanding precisely what material object the legislator meant to assign to the phrase of *manifestation of conscience* as employed in canon 530.

1) *The Quasi-Sacramental Manifestation of Conscience*

This first type of manifestation involves the revelation of sins, whether already absolved or yet to be absolved, and of lesser moral faults, failings, and imperfections. This quasi-sacramental manifestation has as its specific object those matters which are proper to sacramental confession and which are most difficult to reveal by reason of the shame and humiliation involved. The revelation of such matter constitutes a manifestation of conscience in the strictest sense.

There is no doubt that the legislator strictly forbids superiors to elicit this type of manifestation. Even during the era when the mandatory and elicited manifestation was in vogue, superiors were forbidden to infringe upon the sphere of the confessor. This is clearly indicated in the preamble of *Quemadmodum,* which sets forth the reasons underlying its restrictive norms:

> For, inasmuch as occasionally their Constitutions permitted the making of a manifestation of conscience, in order that thereby the members might the more easily learn, in their doubts, from experienced superiors, how to walk in the path of perfection, it has happened on the contrary, that some of the latter have introduced the practice of thoroughly inquiring into the state of their subjects' conscience, which is a thing reserved exclusively to the sacrament of penance.[22]

A careful reading of this text shows that an elicited manifestation of conscience, prescinding from sin, had been permitted prior to *Quemadmodum.* Even during this period, which favored and urged the manifestation, it was considered a serious abuse for superiors to inquire about matter proper to the sacrament of penance. In the light of the intervening restrictive legislation of *Quemadmodum,* it is all the more evident that canon 530 must categorically proscribe any eliciting of the quasi-sacramental manifestation.

2) *The Ascetical Manifestation of Conscience*

The specific material object of this type of manifestation has a positive and negative phase, and, like the quasi-sacramental manifestation, is concerned with matters of the greatest intimacy. Positively, the ascetical manifestation embraces hidden, interior acts of virtue, victories over temptations, special graces, lights and good intentions. Negatively, it includes such elements as temptations, propensities to evil, improper attractions and deep personal repugnances. The revelation of these matters for the sake of direction constitutes a manifestation of conscience in the strict sense.

Since there was never any legal doubt about the proscription of the quasi-sacramental manifestation in the pre-*Quemadmodum* period, the

[22] *Fontes,* n. 2017; Sabetti, *The Decree,* p. 6.

abrogation contained in the decree can only have been directed towards a less intimate type of manifestation. The terms of the decree are general but sufficiently clear:

> His Holiness annuls, abrogates, and declares of no force whatever all regulations whatsoever in the constitutions ... in this one point in which these constitutions regard the secret manifestation of heart and conscience in whatever manner or under what name soever.[23]

As these words are directed towards the abolishment of "the secret manifestation of heart and conscience," (the decree already assuming the prohibition to enter upon confessional matter), it must necessarily be concluded that the law forbids all inquiries concerning the negative and positive matters of intimate conscience proper to the ascetical manifestation. Therefore, since the Code reproduces the former legislation on this point, canon 530 must likewise be understood as prohibiting the induced ascetical manifestation of conscience.[24]

3) *The Academic Manifestation of Conscience*

This type of manifestation concerns itself with the memory and the intellect rather than with the conscience. Its relevant areas embrace in particular the end-results of the lectures on the religious and spiritual life, and in general the whole formation program in force for the young religious. Its material object is academic and abstract, rather than of a purely personal and concrete nature. The academic manifestation would provide a framework for inquiries on the understanding of the religious state, the traditions and spirit of the institutes, and on the concepts of poverty, chastity, and obedience. This final type of manifestation is evidently not as intimate as the quasi-sacramental and

[23]*Fontes*, n. 2017; Sabetti, *The Decree*, p. 11. The translation which has been cited throughout renders "... cordis et conscientiae intimam manifestationem ..." simply as "secret manifestation of conscience."

[24]Creusen-Ellis divide the manifestation of conscience into the strict and broad manifestation and state that it is the strict manifestation which is forbidden by the law. The matter of this strict manifestation corresponds very closely to that of both the quasi-sacramental and ascetical manifestation of the present work. The definition of the strict manifestation as given by these authors makes this clear: "to manifest one's conscience means to reveal one's hidden faults with their degree of culpability, one's hidden acts of virtue, one's intentions, the affections and repugnances to which one has yielded, the temptations or trials which God sends, the lights and good desires received from Him."—*Religious Men and Women*, n. 128.

ascetical manifestation. It is only by a certain extension of the terminology that it can be labelled a manifestation of conscience at all.

This type of manifestation is not forbidden by the law. Canon 565, §1, states that the object of the novitiate year is:

> the forming of the mind of the novices by means of study of the rule and constitutions, by pious meditations and assiduous prayer, by instructions on those matters which pertain to vows and virtues, by suitable exercises in rooting out the germs of vice, in regulating the motives of soul, in acquiring virtues.

This formation is to be given under the direction of the master of novices. In order to check the results of his efforts, he must be able to ask certain questions of his charges. He may not exact or elicit the quasi-sacramental or ascetical manifestation of conscience, but he certainly may inquire about the less intimate and more general matters—matters which might be considered academic for novices and young religious who truly are students of the spiritual life. On this point Sabetti aptly remarks: "... Masters and Mistresses of novices may inquire if their *instructions* on the different acts of piety and exercises of the spiritual life were properly *understood*."[25] Thus, questions about the school of spirituality preferred; the meaning of such concepts as particular friendship, reverential fear, scrupulosity, perfect chastity; as well as the means of avoiding the common pitfalls of religious life, are not at all out of place. In practice, there will be borderline cases, where the superior might do best to gain the full confidence of the subject and thereby a full spontaneous manifestation, rather than violate in any way the rights of conscience which the law is so determined to safeguard.

In fine, by the term *manifestation of conscience* the legislator includes both the quasi-sacramental and ascetical manifestations. The law, therefore, forbids superiors to induce their subjects to reveal to them sins, faults, imperfections, weaknesses, propensities to evil, special repugnances and attractions, good intentions, secret acts of virtue, special lights and graces, and similar matters of an intimate, personal nature. This will be the denotation of the expression *manifestation of conscience* whenever it occurs hereafter without any qualification.

[25] *The Decree*, p. 7.

CHAPTER V
COMMENTARY ON §1 OF CANON 530

The text of canon 530, §1, reads: "All religious superiors are strictly forbidden to induce in any manner persons subject to them to make a manifestation of conscience to them." The present chapter offers a detailed analysis of the various elements in the foregoing prescription.

ARTICLE 1: "RELIGIOUS SUPERIORS"

The most serious problem presented by canon 530 arises from the difficulty of circumscribing the precise meaning of the expression, *religious superiors,* in this particular frame of reference. At no point in the Code is there to be found a formal, juridical definition of this term. Canon 501, §1, simply states that superiors are those who have dominative power over those persons who are subject to them.[1] If they are clerical exempt religious, these superiors possess in addition true ecclesiastical jurisdiction. The Code applies the title of superior only to those religious who belong to the internal hierarchy of an Institute and govern the entire Institute, a number of its foundations, or an individual foundation, as well as those who by law or appointment take their place. Such would include the supreme, provincial or local moderator, visitator, vice-provincial, vice-rector or vicar, prior in an abbey, and sub-prior in a priory.[2] By the same token, the Code does not apply the term *religious superior* to those non-members who have qualified authority over the religious.[3] Such would include local ordinaries and their delegates (e.g., vicars for religious, visitators, examiners of candidates for reception or profession).[4]

It is certain that the prohibition of canon 530 does not apply to local ordinaries and their delegates, for although these can be superiors of

[1] Dominative power is that which is exercised over subjects in view of their profession.

[2] Creusen-Ellis, *Religious Men and Women,* n. 130.—Religious superiors may be prelates, clerics, lay men, or lay women.

[3] Canon 500, §1.

[4] Larraona, "Commentarium Codicis," *CpR,* XII (1931), 126.

religious, they are not religious superiors in the strict sense of the word.[5] With equal certainty the prohibition does apply to general, provincial, and local moderators, and their vicars. However, it remains to be determined whether the term *religious superior* as used by the canon, is susceptible of a broad interpretation in virtue of which the prohibition in question must be extended to such officials as exercise only social or domestic authority in a community (e.g., novice masters and prefects of students).

Most authors, it will be seen, interpret the term in question in a strict sense and thereby restrict the prohibition of canon 530 to superiors properly so-called. Some authors, however, interpret the term, *religious superior,* in a broad manner, and in turn extend the prohibition of the canon to lesser officials, such as the master of novices and prefect of students.

To obviate possible confusion, it should be explicitly noted that the strict interpretation of the term, *religious superior,* will have as its end-result a broad interpretation of the canon as a whole, because it will confine the prohibition in question to a more limited number: viz., only to superiors properly so-called. By the same standard, the broad interpretation of the term, *religious superior,* in the present context will have as its end-result a strict interpretation of the canon as a whole, because it will extend the prohibition to a wider number: namely, to officials such as novice masters and prefects of students, as well as to superiors properly so-called. Therefore, a process which might be described as one of inverse proportionality is at issue. Both interpretations will now be examined in detail. For purposes of convenience, the first view (i.e., the opinion which limits the number of those affected by the prohibition to superiors properly so-called) will be labeled the *Restrictive Interpretation.* The second position (i.e., the view which extends the prohibition to masters of novices and prefects of students) will be designated the *Extensive Interpretation.*

[5]This does not imply that local ordinaries may constrain religious to make a manifestation of conscience to them. Both *Quemadmodum* and the canon aimed at stemming the abuses caused by those constitutions and Rules which commanded the manifestation to be made to religious superiors. Only such superiors, according to the particular law, had the right to exact the manifestation. Therefore, it was only from these that the Church had to rescind the right.

Section 1: *The Restrictive Interpretation*

According to canon 18, the first rule of legal interpretation consists in examining the proper meaning of the words of a given canon in relevant context. Title X of Book II of the Code, *De religionum regimine,* under which canon 530 is found, treats of strict government. Hence its preoccupation with superiors in the strict sense. When the canon says *ALL religious superiors,* therefore, it does not mean superiors in both the strict and broad sense, but rather all superiors in the strict sense, whether these superiors be clerical or lay, male or female.[6] Creusen-Ellis say that by *superiors* here must be understood those to whom the Code accords that title, i.e., those who govern the institute, provinces, or houses. "The definitions of the Code," these authors continue, "ought to be applied strictly, unless there is proof to the contrary, or we shall be in danger of falling into arbitrary judgments."[7]

The vast majority of authors maintain that the words *religious superiors,* as used in canon 530, must be interpreted strictly, so as to include only superiors properly so-called. Thus, Fanfani remarks that *superiors* here must be so understood as not to include novice masters.[8] Regatillo equates the term with those who have authority over the whole community, thus excluding such officials as the master of novices.[9] Larraona is of the opinion that the canon certainly includes every superior, supreme, provincial and local, whether male or female, but it excludes those who, although exercising some authority, are not superiors strictly so-called in law, namely, the novice master and student prefect.[10] Voltas is committed to the view that the words *all religious superiors* include generals, provincials, quasi-provincials, abbots, local superiors. These, he declares, are superiors in the proper sense of the word, and adds that novice masters and prefects of students are not included by

[6]Fanfani, *De Iure Religiosorum Ad Normam Codicis Iuris Canonici* (3 ed., Rovigo: Istituto Pandano di Arti Grafiche, 1949), n. 132 (hereafter cited *De Iure Religiosorum*).

[7]*Religious Men and Women,* n. 130.

[8]*De Iure Religiosorum,* n. 132.

[9]*Institutiones Iuris Canonici* (5 ed., 2 vols., Santander: Editorial Sal Terrae, 1956), I, n. 679 (hereafter cited *Institutiones*).

[10]"Commentarium Codicis," *CpR,* XII (1931), p. 126.

the letter of the law.[11] Schaefer,[12] Vermeersch-Creusen,[13] Papi,[14] and a number of other authors hold the same opinion.[15] Wernz-Vidal correctly affirm that this is the common opinion of the authors.[16]

However, most of these manualists are in agreement that, while the novice master, for instance, is not included under the letter of the law, he is bound by its spirit, in that he is not allowed to force or constrain the novices to manifest the state of their conscience to him. These authors maintain that the master is forbidden to force or demand the novices to make the manifestation, but is not forbidden to commend or even urge the practice.[17] Thus, Schaefer argues that since canon 530 does not bind the master of novices, he can induce or urge the manifestation but cannot command or force it.[18] Goyeneche permits the novice master to commend the practice to the novices, by virtue of the fact that he is not a religious superior in the strict sense. Since the master's relationship to the novices, he adds, is not the same as that of a superior to his subjects, there is no need of applying to him the letter of the law of canon 530.[19]

Several of these commentators contend that the novice master must not only refrain from demanding the manifestation of conscience from the novices, but must even avoid showing displeasure to those novices who do not freely make this manifestation to him. Therefore, in commending the practice, the master should not praise those who make use of it, nor should he magnify the dangers to those who forgo its use.[20]

[11]"De Aperienda, Directionis Causa, Superioribus Conscientia," *CpR,* I (1920), p. 148 (hereafter cited "De Aperienda").

[12]*De Religiosis,* p. 365, n. 687.

[13]*Epitome,* I, n. 650.

[14]*Religious in Church Law* (New York: Kenedy, 1924), p. 160.

[15]Cf. Huysmans, *La Manifestation de Conscience en Religion, d-apres le Canon* 530 (Lovanii: Bibliotheca Alphonsiana, 1953), p. 76, for an exhaustive list of authors holding the Restrictive Interpretation.

[16]*Ius Canonicum,* III, n. 213.

[17]Fanfani, *De Iure Religiosorum,* n. 208; Wernz-Vidal, *Ius Canonicum,* III, n. 213; Voltas, "De Aperienda," *CpR,* I (1920), p. 150.

[18]*De Religiosis,* p. 511, n. 903.

[19]"Consultatio," *CpR,* V (1924), pp. 160-161.

[20]Wernz-Vidal, *Ius Canonicum,* III, n. 213; Fanfani, *De Iure Religiosorum,* n. 208.

Finally, these authors unanimously agree that, while not forbidden to induce the manifestation, the superior must avoid any question or point relating to areas proper to sacramental confession.[21] Creusen-Ellis may be cited as their spokesmen:

> Even though the prohibition expressed in canon 530 is not intended for them, still it is certainly forbidden to masters of novices to demand the secret manifestation of conscience, that is to say, of anything which comes within the domain of the sacrament of penance.[22]

In summation, the Restrictive Interpretation excludes from the term *religious superiors* officials such as the novice master and prefect of students, and would assign these latter the following functions with reference to the manifestation: 1) permission to urge and encourage the ascetical manifestation of conscience; 2) prohibition to command the ascetical manifestation; 3) prohibition to elicit the quasi-sacramental manifestation in any manner.

It is the contention of the present writer that the Restrictive Interpretation offers an incorrect analysis of canon 530, by virtue of the limitation it reads into the expression *religious superiors*. Before presenting the arguments in defense of this contrary view, to which the present writer subscribes, a number of objections against the Restrictive Interpretation must be considered.

At the outset, the Restrictive Interpretation forbids superiors as well as officials from resorting to any persuasion or constraint in eliciting the manifestation from their subjects. Schaefer, for instance, asserts that the master cannot constrain the novices to make the manifestation.[23] Creusen-Ellis state that although the prohibition expressed in canon 530, §1, is not intended for masters of novices, it is certainly forbidden them to demand the manifestation of conscience from their subjects.[24] According to the same Restrictive Interpretation, however, canon 530 purposely excludes novice masters and prefects of students from its prohibition, in order to safeguard the efficacious fulfillment of their twofold function of forming and educating young religious. Therefore,

21 Schaefer, *De Religiosis*, p. 511, n. 903; Vermeersch-Creusen, *Epitome*, I, n. 650; Wernz-Vidal, *Ius Canonicum*, III, n. 213.

22 *Religious Men and Women*, n. 130.

23 *De Religiosis*, p. 366, n. 689; p. 511, n. 903.

24 *Religious Men and Women*, n. 130.

consistency would seem to demand that this interpretation should allow these officials to insist on the manifestation whenever they deem this necessary for the fulfillment of their duty.[25]

Although the Restrictive Interpretation forbids novice masters, prefects of students and similar officials to use force in soliciting the manifestation of conscience, it permits these officials to encourage and urge their subjects to make the manifestation to them.[26] This occasions a second objection: it gives rise to a danger which the legislator was at pains to prevent—namely, the use of constraint. When an official with domestic or social power in the community, e.g., the novice master or prefect of students, urges his subjects to make a manifestation to him, the danger of moral force most assuredly becomes a realistic factor. This danger will be present especially in houses of formation. Novices and young professed religious, by reason of their reluctance to displease the master or prefect, would in practice hardly be at liberty to reject the latter's recommendation. Even if the master or prefect urges the making of a manifestation in a moderate way, the mere fact that this recommendation comes from a person in authority applies moral force to the more sensitive subjects. Hence, a resultant manifestation would be motivated by true moral force, or at least by reverential fear. It is also conceivable that some of these subjects, fearing to displease one in authority and simultaneously ashamed to make a true manifestation, will approach the master or prefect with a spiritual self-revelation which is formalistic or even false.

The danger of undue persuasion through moral force will not be present, of course, if in counseling the manifestation in a general way, the master or prefect suggests that it could be made to one's confessor or any priest counsellor. In this case, the subjects are free, since the master or prefect will not know who is accepting and who is rejecting his proposal. It is clear that the subject who presents himself to the master or prefect as a result of such a general recommendation will be doing so freely and spontaneously as the law desires.[27]

A third inconsistency of the Restrictive Interpretation is seen in its exemption of novice masters and student prefects from the prohibi-

[25]Huysmans, *La Manifestation de Conscience en Religion*, p. 78.

[26]Fanfani, *De Iure Religiosorum*, n. 208; Wernz-Vidal, *Ius Canonicum*, III, n. 213; Voltas, "De Aperienda," *CpR*, I (1920), p. 150.

[27]Canon 530, §2.

tion of canon 530, while simultaneously forbidding these same officials from eliciting the quasi-sacramental manifestation in any manner.[28] If an intimate manifestation of conscience is so necessary for proper direction, and the Code (as the Restrictive Interpretation maintains) has therefore seen fit to exempt novice masters and prefects of students from the canon, how can this interpretation afford to exclude the matter of confession, in which area are found the most genuine and least deceitful elements conducive to effective spiritual guidance? There are many cases where an adequate manifestation cannot be made, nor adequate direction given, unless the most intimate matters of conscience are revealed, that is, unless there is made what in effect amounts to a quasi-sacramental manifestation. For example, according to the Restrictive Interpretation, novice masters and student prefects can induce a subject to make a manifestation of temptations, since these latter in themselves belong to the ascetical, not to the quasi-sacramental manifestation. But it is at this point that these officials must terminate the series of questions. Were they to ask the logical, ensuing questions as to whether or not the said temptations had been consented to, they would be entering the forbidden sphere of the quasi-sacramental manifestation. The value of such a partial manifestation is certainly questionable.

Creusen's statement that novice masters are not bound by canon 530 in virtue of the canon's position in the Code occasions a final objection against this opinion. Canon 530 is found in Title X of Book II which treats of the government of Religious Institutes (*De religionum regimine*). In stating that the novice master is not bound by canon 530, Creusen cites this title and seems to imply that since it treats only of strict government, it refers only to superiors in the strict sense.[29] However, Chapter II of the Title in question treats of confessors and chaplains (*De confessariis et cappellanis*), and in no sense of the word can these be considered superiors. Since they, too, are treated in Title X, Book II, of the Code, it is not unreasonable that a reference to officials such as masters of novices and prefects of students occur there also.

In conclusion, the Restrictive Interpretation exempts novice masters and prefects of students from the proscription of canon 530, but it is to

[28]Schaefer, *De Religiosis*, p. 511, n. 903; Vermeersch-Creusen, *Epitome*, I, n. 650; Wernz-Vidal, *Ius Canonicum*, III, n. 213; Creusen-Ellis, *Religious Men and Women*, n. 130.

[29]*Epitome*, I, n. 713.

be urged that the liberty thus afforded them in theory is actually so limited as to render it virtually ineffectual in most instances. On the one hand, this interpretation allows novice masters and prefects of students to elicit the ascetical manifestation, but on the other, it restrains them from demanding the ascetical manifestation, and *a fortiori* forbids them to induce the quasi-sacramental manifestation in any manner. Therefore, for all effects and purposes, this opinion veers close to the opposing Extensive Interpretation which insists that masters and prefects, over and above superiors properly so-called, are bound by the prohibition of canon 530. Ultimately, the only difference between the two is that the Restrictive Opinion allows masters and prefects to elicit the ascetical manifestation, while the Extensive Interpretation denies them even this right. The Extensive Interpretation agrees that the Church beyond all shadow of doubt takes cognizance of the value of the manifestation of conscience as a powerful aid in spiritual direction. However, this opinion prefers to interpret this recognition in terms not of a partial exemption for novice masters and prefects of students from canon 530, but rather by way of a general approval of the free and spontaneous manifestation of conscience. This, it seems to the present writer, is the more logical and defensible approach.

Section 2: *Extensive Interpretation*

This position is based on the contention that canon 530 is not an entirely new law, but merely repeats an old law. Therefore, to understand its full meaning, canon 530 must be interpreted in the light of *Quemadmodum.*[30]

It is the basic contention of the Extensive Interpretation that masters of novices and prefects of students were just as responsible for the abuses condemned by the decree as were superiors in the strict sense. This interpretation considers psychologically unrealistic the allegation that in institutes where the obligatory manifestation of conscience had been legally authorized, only superiors in the strict sense were guilty of abuses, while novice masters and prefects of students had never fallen short of the dictates of prudence and delicacy. Hence, in his attempt to eradicate these abuses, there is little justification in deducing that the legislator distinguished or meant to distinguish between superiors in the strict sense and these officials. It would be a cause for wonderment

[30]Canon 6, nos. 2, 3, 4.

if the Church, desiring to uproot the evils connected with the manifestation, should have introduced a distinction which would have frustrated her very purpose.[31] Therefore, it is the considered judgment of this second school of thought that *Quemadmodum* prohibited officials, such as masters of novices and prefects of students from eliciting the manifestation of conscience in any way.

The Extensive opinion appeals to the separate texts of *Quemadmodum* with its dependent jurisprudence and its commentators, and of canon 530 with its corresponding jurisprudence and commentators, to prove its contention.

As for the text of *Quemadmodum* itself, the opening norm reads as follows:

> His Holiness abrogates ... all dispositions of constitutions ... so far as they regard the secret manifestation of conscience in whatsoever manner or under any name whatever. He, therefore, seriously enjoins on all superiors ... to absolutely cancel and expunge altogether from their respective Constitutions, Directories, and Manuals, all the aforesaid regulations. Likewise, He annuls and abolishes all contrary usages and customs even immemorial.[32]

The language of the law is general and leaves no room for exceptions. The legislator is not merely prohibiting superiors from inducing the manifestation, he is abrogating the obligatory and solicited manifestation as such. Superiors are commanded to expunge from the constitutions, directories, and manuals, all regulations concerning the manifestation. No distinction is made regarding the recipients of the manifestation. Since the implementation of this law requires the deletion of all dispositions concerning the manifestation contained in the Rules, directories, or books of customs for novices and religious students, it must be inferred that *Quemadmodum* binds masters of novices and prefects of students as well as superiors in the strict sense of the word.[33]

Quemadmodum also imposed the obligation of inserting the entire decree into the constitutions, and demanded its public reading once a year. The condemnation and abrogation of the manifestation would have provoked unlimited confusion for the novices and young professed, if they were still bound to make the manifestation to their masters and prefects. This confirms the contention that *Quemadmodum* applied not

[31]Huysmans, *La Manifestation de Conscience en Religion*, p. 64.

[32]*Fontes*, n. 2017; Sabetti, *The Decree*, p. 11.

[33]Sabetti, *The Decree*, p. 11.

only to superiors in the strict sense but also to masters of novices and prefects of students.

As for the jurisprudence dependent on *Quemadmodum,* this is most clearly summarized in the Norms of 1901 issued by the Sacred Congregation of Bishops and Regulars.[34] No. 79 of these Norms expressly prohibits mistresses of novices as well as directresses of institutes from eliciting the manifestation of conscience from their subjects:

> They are not bound to manifest the state of their consciences to the mistress of novices, nor to the moderators of the Institute, nor are they bound to render an account of their past life, nor can they be induced to do this (decree *Quemadmodum*).[35]

This norm is important for the interpretation of the decree and indirectly also for the interpretation of canon 530, for it places mistresses of novices on a par with superiors in the strict sense as regards the manifestation of conscience. This testimony strengthens the argument already based on the text of the decree itself.

A survey of the commentaries of the decree reveals that many pre-Code authors, especially after the Norms of 1901, argued that *Quemadmodum* bound officials such as the novice master. Pius of Langogne, in his extensive commentary on *Quemadmodum,* states that the text of the decree excludes all restrictions and consequently includes novitiates in its prohibition. He adds that the disposition of the decree permitting subjects freely to approach their superiors should fully appease those who fear that the formation of the novices will suffer as a result of the abrogation of the obligatory and elicited manifestation of conscience.[36] Sabetti, in commenting on the decree, writes that just as superiors in the strict sense are limited to inquiries about external faults, so novice

[34]*Normae Secundum Quas S. Congr. Episcoporum et Regularium Procedere Solet in Approbandis Novis Institutis Votorum Simplicium* (Romae, 1901), (hereafter cited *Norms of* 1901); Schaefer, *De Religiosis,* Appendix II, p. 1102.

[35]"Non tenentur tamen suae conscientiae statum manifestum facere magistrae novitiarum, nec moderatricibus Instituti, neque ipsis anteactae vitae suae rationem reddere, neque ad hoc induci possunt (decr. *Quemadmodum*)."—*Loc. cit.*

"In ... normis de sororibus quidem potissimum sermo est; ea autem quae de ipsis dicuntur, etiam religiosis viris applicantur, his exceptis: solas sorores respiciunt n. 64, 65, 80, 81, 91-95, 139-147, 149, 171, 172, 173, 178, 224; solos autem viros n. 58, 201, 324, 325; cf. Schaefer *De Religiosis,* Appendix II, p. 1102.

[36]*L'Ouverture de Conscience, les Confessions et Communions dans les Communautes* (Paris, 1891), pp. 48, 102.

masters are restricted to questions on the effects of their conferences.[37] Likewise, Arndt, in his study of *Quemadmodum*, affirms explicitly that masters of novices and directors of postulants, as well as superiors, are certainly bound to observe the norms set down by the decree.[38] Piat holds that novices are included by the decree and for proof singles out No. 79 of the Norms of 1901.[39] Franco, one of the first commentators on the decree, cites the question of a superioress or mistress of novices who wished to know if novices were subject to the decree, and if she could still ask such questions as: "Have you anxieties of conscience?" and "Are you tempted against chastity?" He replies that novices are evidently included by the decree, and that since the questions at hand intrude upon the domain of conscience, they may not be employed by such officials.[40]

This examination of the old legislation, its jurisprudence and its commentators, sufficiently substantiates the validity of the Extensive Interpretation prior to the Code. A parallel analysis of canon 530 with its jurisprudence and commentators will yield the same result.

As for the text of canon 530, §1, the Code employs the same broad terminology as the decree, namely, *religious superiors*. The wording of the canon gives no indication of any warranted restrictions as to the interpretation of this term. *Quemadmodum* had exempted superiors of clerical religious institutes, but with canon 530 the common law eliminates even this exemption. This application of the discipline to clerical as well as lay institutes indicates that the legislator did not intend to narrow the general character of the law which had been in force within the institutes bound by *Quemadmodum*. It would be absurd had the legislator extended the prohibition to clerical religious on the one hand, and exempted the lay masters and prefects who had been bound by *Quemadmodum*, on the other. There is no historical evidence to the effect that circumstances so changed from the time of the decree to that of the codification of Church law, to justify exempting some of those who had been included by the prohibition of the decree. Canon 530,

[37] *The Decree*, p. 7.

[38] "Das Decret *Quemadmodum* fuer Ordensfrauen und Laiengenossenschaften," *Archiv fuer katholisches Kirchenrecht*, LXXVI (1896), 235-236.

[39] *Praelectiones Iuris Regularium* (3 ed., 3 vols., Tournay: Casterman, 1906), I, 521 (hereafter cited *Praelectiones*).

[40] *Ad Una Superiora*, pp. 30-32.

therefore, does not restrict the meaning of the expression, ***religious superior***. The term continues to have the same broad meaning it had in the decree. In brief, it includes not only superiors in the strict sense, but also masters of novices and prefects of students.

The jurisprudence relative to the present law on the manifestation of conscience finds its best expression in the Norms published by the Sacred Congregation for the Propagation of the Faith, June 29, 1940.[41] No. 81 of these Norms reads: "All superiors and mistresses of novices are strictly forbidden to induce in any manner the sisters subject to them to make a manifestation of conscience to them . . ."[42] The wording of this text places the mistress of novices on the same plane as the superioress with reference to the manifestation of conscience. Such officials are again forbidden with the same force as superiors in the strict sense to elicit a manifestation of conscience from their subjects. The wording of this statement of the Congregation reflects dependence on canon 530 and accordingly is an important aid in interpreting the canon itself.

An analysis of the commentaries on canon 530 reveals that the majority applies its prohibition only to superiors in the strict sense,[43] and maintains that lesser officials are bound only by its spirit. There are, however, a number of noteworthy commentators who defend the Extensive Interpretation in this regard. Bastien agrees with the majority of authors that the novice master is not a superior in the strict sense. Thus, he points out, that if canon 530 is considered in isolation, it must be admitted that the novice master is not bound by the letter of the law. But, he continues, since canon 530, §1 is almost literally the same as the parallel proscription of the decree *Quemadmodum*, and since the jurisprudence of the Sacred Congregation interpreted the words of the decree as applying not only to superiors in the strict sense but also to mistresses and masters of novices, it follows that these latter also fall under the negative imposition of the Code law.[44]

[41] *Normae pro Constitutionibus Congregationum Iuris Diocesani a S.C. de Propaganda Fide Dependentium* (Romae: Typis Polyglottis Vaticanis, 1940), p. 18 (hereafter cited *Norms of* 1940).

[42] "Superiorissae omnes et magistrae novitiarum districte vetantur sorores sibi subditas quoquo modo inducere ad conscientiae manifestationem sibi peragendam . . ." —*Loc. cit.*

[43] Cf. *supra*, p. 58.

[44] *Directoire Canonique a l'Usage des Congregations a Voeux Simples*, (4 ed., Bruges, 1933), pp. 141-142.

Berutti approaches the problem from another angle. He notes that religious superiors are strictly forbidden to hear habitually the confessions of the persons subject to them without a grave cause,[45] lest difficulties and dangers in the external government of the community arise. For the same reason, he observes, superiors are forbidden to induce their subjects to make a manifestation of conscience to them. In parallel fashion, Berutti points out, novice masters are strictly forbidden to hear the confessions of the novices who are subject to them.[46] Therefore, he concludes, canon 530 must be applied with equal cogency to novice masters and prefects of students, as to superiors in the strict sense. He admits that the novice master is certainly not a superior in the strict sense, but makes the point that canon 530, §1, is established for all religious superiors in relation to those persons who are subject to them. Hence the novice master cannot be excluded.[47]

Chelodi-Ciprotti aver that although officials such as novice masters and prefects of students are not superiors in the strict sense, they are nevertheless affected by canon 530 in view of the purpose of the law. Canon 530 cannot achieve its objective, namely, freedom of conscience for religious subjects, if novice masters and prefects of students are free to induce their subjects to make the manifestation. Therefore, these joint authors conclude, such officials are certainly obligated by the prohibition of canon 530.[48]

The basic argument for the Extensive Interpretation rests on the fact that the Code law is substantially a repetition of the old law of *Quemadmodum*. Hence canon 530 must be interpreted within the juridical context of that decree. But *Quemadmodum* clearly bound novice masters and prefects of students as well as superiors in the strict sense. There-

[45]Canon 518, §2.

[46]Canon 891.

[47]*Institutiones Iuris Canonici* (6 vols., Vol. III, Taurini-Romae: Marietti, 1936), III, 109.

[48]*Ius Canonicum de Personis* (3 ed., Vincenza: Società Anonima Tipografica, 1942), p. 408.—Other present day authors also hold to this opinion, e.g., Lover, *The Master of Novices*, The Catholic University of America Canon Law Studies, n. 254 (Washington, D.C.: The Catholic University of America Press, 1947), p. 105; Huysmans, *La Manifestation de Conscience en Religion*, pp. 82-83. Gutierrez concludes that the novice master is bound not by reason of the letter of the law but through a certain juridical analogy, "De Manifestatione Conscientiae et Directione Spirituali in Religione," *CpRM*, XXXIV (1954), 170-171.

fore, canon 530 must likewise exert its proscriptive force upon these officials.

There are two basic objections which are leveled against the Extensive Interpretation of canon 530. It seems to the present writer that both can be answered thoroughly and cogently.

The first objection centers on whether canon 530 is an odious or a favorable law. If the canon is viewed from the standpoint of superiors it is seen as an odious law, one which limits the free exercise of a right of superiors, and therefore a law to be restricted to as few superiors as possible. This point of perspective is directly opposed to that of the Extensive Interpretation which approaches the matter at issue from the subjects' standpoint, and therefore prefers to regard this as a favorable law. Hence, the prohibition of the canon is to be extended to as many superiors as possible. Authors who consider the canon from this latter viewpoint maintain that it restores and safeguards the freedom of conscience of subjects and therefore merits broad interpretation.[49] This, it seems to the present writer, is the more reasonable approach. This point is susceptible of further development.

Man as a social being is responsible for all his externally detectable infractions of the law of society. Man as a free and reasonable creature must, moreover, answer to God not only for his social failings but for his thoughts and actions, even the most intimate and secret. To God alone, the Supreme Judge, he cannot refuse to lay open any of the recesses of his conscience. On the contrary, no human being has the right *per se* to search the depths of the conscience of another. In the name of the natural law every man has a right to his innermost secrets. The only exceptions to this rule arise from the expressed will of God or from the free consent of the man involved, who can yield his right should it seem advantageous to him. Just as a man may cede his natural right to marry by a vow of celibacy, so in like manner he may by free consent cede the right to complete freedom of conscience. This condition is verified when a man submits himself to a law which restrains the free exercise of such a natural right. Now a law which curbs the free exercise of a right,—in the present case a natural right—is a law to be interpreted strictly. Therefore, the pre-*Quemadmodum* religious Rules and constitutions which commanded the manifestation of con-

[49]Huysmans, *La Manifestation de Conscience en Religion,* p. 60; Lover, *The Master of Novices,* pp. 97-98.—Franco, *Ad Una Superiora,* pp. 30-31, interpreted *Quemadmodum* from the same point of view.

science must be considered as laws to be interpreted strictly. When an ensuing law suppresses such an earlier law, it restores to the individuals the free exercise of their natural rights. As a result, the subsequent legislation is to be broadly interpreted as a favorable law which has restored natural liberty. Such is the case in the present legislation embodied in canon 530, §1, with reference to the Rules and constitutions which had demanded the manifestation. Therefore, the canon is to be interpreted broadly, that is, in favor of the subject. Consequently, it is to include as many as possible of those in authority under its prohibition.

A second objection which is raised against the Extensive Interpretation stems from and stresses the difficulty which officials such as the novice master and prefect of students would have in forming their charges in the religious life, were they not able to elicit the manifestation.[50] In the first place, this objection is weakened by the concessions on the part of the Restrictive Interpretation which forbid the master and prefect from demanding the manifestation of conscience and from eliciting in any way a quasi-sacramental manifestation of conscience.[51] Second, it must be noted that the intimate direction of the young religious is neither the principal, nor the proper and exclusive duty of the master or prefect. Hence the position that these officials must be able to elicit the manifestation in order to fulfill the duties of their office is not legally sound.[52]

Two distinct tasks, namely, the formation in the religious life, on the one side, and intimate spiritual direction, on the other, merge in the training of the young religious. It is a confusion of these tasks which give rise to the present objection. Canons 565, §1, and 588, §1, set forth the basic regulations concerning formation in the religious life. These canons oblige the master and prefect to provide by suitable means for the proper formation of their charges throughout the period of training. They are to form and educate these young religious according to the end of the institute, its Rule, constitutions, customs, traditions, and spirit. All of these duties can be discharged without recourse to the manifestation of conscience. The Code, however, refrains from regulating intimate spiritual direction. The law makes it clear that masters are not the official

[50]Wernz-Vidal, *Ius Canonicum,* III, n. 283.

[51]Cf. *supra,* pp. 59-61.

[52]Goyeneche, "Consultatio," *CpRM,* XVIII (1937), 90-91; Schaefer, *De Religiosis,* p. 511, n. 903.

directors of their subjects' intimate spiritual life when it forbids them to hear the confessions of the novices, except in grave and urgent cases in which they are spontaneously approached.[53]

The absence of positive norms relative to intimate spiritual direction reflects the mind of the Church that such direction is basically a private matter—a matter of confidence and quite impossible without an adequate manifestation of conscience. Therefore, spiritual writers have always insisted on the free and considered choice of a spiritual director, and on the possibility of changing one's director in certain circumstances. This necessary privacy and freedom would be lost, if hard and fast regulations surrounded intimate spiritual direction. Lover points out that there is not a single word in the entire section of the Code on the novice master which indicates that he is to be the principal or exclusive moderator of the consciences of the novices who are subject to him.[54] Even in those instances where a determined individual is appointed as an official spiritual director, he by no means becomes the one and only person to whom all must go for such direction. Rather he is the director available by reason of his office to those who freely address themselves to him for the purpose of guidance.

A clear understanding of the distinction between these two tasks, namely, the formation in the religious life, on the one hand, and intimate spiritual direction, on the other, disposes of the objection that novice masters and prefects of students cannot fulfill their duties without eliciting the manifestation of conscience. This distinction, envisioned by the legislator, enables these officials to carry out their assigned tasks effectively, while at the same time being bound by the letter of the law of canon 530. They can question their charges about everything which refers to their office of providing formation and instruction, while refraining from entering upon the terrain of the confessor and spiritual director. These officials can describe the practice of the manifestation of conscience and can explain its advantages and limitations. Moreover, they can recommend the practice in a general way, suggesting that it can be made to any competent person, e.g., confessors or spiritual directors. Should the subjects approach the master or prefect to make a manifestation of conscience, as a result of these instructions, such a

[53]Canon 891.

[54]*The Master of Novices*, p. 107.

manifestation will be entirely free and unconstrained, and hence in accord with the Church's law.[55]

Conclusion

In view of the arguments adduced, it seems to the present writer that the Extensive Interpretation of the term, *religious superiors* in canon 530, has more to recommend it. The prohibition to induce the manifestation would, it seems, lose much of its practical force if novice masters and prefects of students were not subject to it. These officials often have far more direct and frequent contact with novices and religious students than do superiors properly so-called. Therefore, if the freedom of conscience of these young religious is to be thoroughly safeguarded by the law, it must be concluded that the master of novices and prefect of students and similar officials with at least social or domestic power are strictly bound by the prohibition of canon 530, §1.

ARTICLE 2: "ALL RELIGIOUS SUPERIORS"

The present article will first offer a very brief commentary on the modifier *all,* occurring in the phrase at hand. This will be followed by a full treatment, both in principle and practice, of the obligation of secrecy binding *all religious superiors* when they receive a free and spontaneous manifestation of conscience.

Section 1: *Commentary*

The word *all* is not found in the decree *Quemadmodum,* since this law was limited to lay religious institutes. Canon 530, §1, on the other hand, by means of the word *all,* encloses within the prohibition of inducing the manifestation the totality of superiors, whether of clerical religious or lay religious institutes. Furthermore, this generalization of the proscription also brings superiors of societies of men and of women living in common without public vows within its ambit. This is clear from canon 675, which states that provisions for the government for each quasi-religious society are to be determined by its own constitutions, but always in compliance with the prescriptions of canons 499-530 insofar as these are applicable.

[55]Canon 530, §2.

Section 2: Obligation of Secrecy

While the Code law forbids the superiors and officials considered above from inducing their subjects to make the manifestation of conscience to them, it by no means denies these subjects the option of making the manifestation freely and spontaneously to their superiors.[56] Therefore, the obligation of secrecy which binds such superiors when they receive a free and spontaneous manifestation of conscience becomes a serious consideration. Two questions present themselves: to what extent are these superiors obliged not to reveal the knowledge received, and to what extent are they obliged *not to make* use of the knowledge received. Each of these will be given general consideration first, and then more explicit analysis by way of a number of pertinent examples.

The knowledge resulting from the manifestation of conscience is classified as a natural and committed secret. This knowledge results from a revelation of the innermost life of a person—the thoughts, feelings, and inclinations which are entirely hidden from others. The manifestation of such intimate matters is made with the implicit understanding that secrecy will be observed. There is no explicit law in the Code concerning the revelation of knowledge acquired outside the confessional. Hence it is necessary to resort to general moral principles to discover the obligation incumbent upon the possessor of such secret knowledge.

A secret, subjectively considered, is the obligation of not revealing some hidden matter; objectively considered, it is the hidden matter itself. A secret may be of three distinct types: natural, promised, or committed. The basis of this traditional classification derives from the source upon which the moral imperativeness of its observance rests. A *natural secret* is one whose obligation arises from the very nature of the matter involved. This matter will be such that it cannot be disclosed without causing some injury to another. A *promised secret* is one whose obligation arises from one's word of honor to safeguard knowledge already possessed. A *committed secret* is one whose obligation stems from an agreement by virtue of which a person receives knowledge unknown before, on the expressed or tacit condition that he will keep this information from others. This mutual understanding may be expressed in words, or may be based on a fact from which it is obvious

[56]Canon 530, §2.

that knowledge has been given in secret—as in the case of knowledge imparted to professional men.[57]

Not all committed secrets give rise to the same obligation of non-revelation. For example, a committed secret between two private persons does not impose as severe an obligation as does such a secret entrusted to a person because of his office, since in this latter instance the secrecy must be respected in view of the public good itself.[58] Knowledge received from a manifestation of conscience is a committed secret of the highest kind and hence imposes a very strict obligation. The secret arising from the manifestation is, in fact, sometimes referred to as quasi sacramental.[59]

To reveal a committed secret licitly, it is required that the revelation be necessary as a means of avoiding a proportionately grave danger.[60] To reveal a secret entrusted by reason of office, however, requires a graver cause than to reveal one entrusted to an individual whose status does not involve official capacity. The reason for this, of course, is the damage to the common good which always results when an official violates a confidence. Evidently, sufficient reasons can exist for revealing committed secrets. It is extremely difficult, however, to justify the violation of such a secret when it arises from a manifestation of conscience. At this point it suffices to say that the extensive moral harm which would befall a community suffering the loss of confidence in its spiritual directors, owing to the violation of the secret relating to a manifestation of conscience, effectively rules out every exception to the contrary. This will be further explained shortly by means of pertinent examples.

Equal rigor attaches to the use of such confidential knowledge. Suarez allowed the use of this knowledge both in the interest of the person in question—provided such use did not vex this individual and it was done without violating the secret—and in the interest of society, because such a secret, he maintained, does not oblige to the detriment of the common good.[61] Modern authors, however, are not so liberal. Wernz-

[57]Noldin-Schmitt-Heinzel, *Summa Theologiae Moralis* (31 ed., 3 vols., Oeniponte: Typis et Sumptibus Feliciani Rauch, 1957), II, 666.

[58]Noldin-Schmitt,Heinzel, *Summa Theologiae Moralis,* II. n. 669.

[59]Aertnys-Damen, *Theologia Moralis secundum Doctrinam S. Alphonsi Ligorio Doct. Ecclesiae* (13 ed., 2 vols., Romae: Marietti, 1939), I, n. 1004.

[60]Noldin-Schmitt-Heinzel, *Summa Theologiae Moralis,* II, n. 670.

[61]*Opera Omnia,* XVI bis, 1087-1088.

Vidal, for example, admit that knowledge gained through a manifestation of conscience can be used only when no harm or inconvenience comes to the subject and when no revelation of the secret results.[62] Since the two conditions here set down can hardly ever with certainty be verified in practice, it can be concluded that a morally justified use of such knowledge is virtually impossible. Goyeneche favors this strict position and offers a few illustrations. The superior, and in particular the novice master and prefect of students, he maintains, cannot use such knowledge in the course of the formal examination which precedes the admission of their subjects to profession or ordination. Nor can the novice master use knowledge revealed to him through the manifestation, in the process of making his report to the higher superiors.[63] Similarly, the discovery of a delict exclusively through the manifestation can never impel the expulsion of a subject, nor give rise to the instituting of a process against him, or even to the admonition of which canon 658, §1, speaks.

A number of representative cases may contribute to the clarification of the principles reviewed above. The following case may be considered first. If a novice master discovers through the manifestation that a novice has a habit of impurity disqualifying him from the religious life and perhaps even endangering the welfare of the community, could he reveal this knowledge to the provincial superior with a view to the novice's dismissal, if after proper exhortation the novice refused to leave?

It might seem at first that a master of novices could bring such knowledge to the attention of the provincial because of the great harm involved. And in fact he might do so, if it were merely a question of weighing the harm threatening the individual novice and that threatening the community and the Church. But a third element enters the case in behalf of the preservation of the secret, that is to say, the element of general confidence attached to the manifestation of conscience as such.[64] The moral harm done to a community by loss of confidence in its spiritual directors is so great that no exception to the secrecy of spiritual direction should be allowed.[65]

[62] *Ius Canonicum,* III, n. 210, note 57.

[63] Goyeneche, "Consultatio," *CpRM,* XVIII (1937), p. 95.

[64] Post, "Novice Master's Obligation to Secrecy," *Review for Religious,* XV (1956), 18-19.

[65] Connell, "A Spiritual Director's Obligation of Secrecy," *American Ecclesiastical*

Two additional cases in point may be considered. The first concerns a religious whose presence constitutes a danger to the community because of his marked influence on a small group. The second case involves a religious who is decisively unworthy of profession or the reception of Orders. Assuming in either case that the facts as stated are certainly true, that they have been ascertained by the spiritual director only through the manifestation of conscience, and that the superiors in ignorance of the facts are contemplating the admission of the person in question to profession or ordination, may the director reveal the offences and the person to the superior in order to prevent grave harm to the community and the Church?

Even in these extraordinary cases, the prefect or master is bound to observe the confidence of the religious students, for he would cause greater harm to the Church by the disclosure of the transgressions than by a silence which would tolerate the admission of an unworthy candidate either to vows or orders. It is true that an evil would be prevented by a word to the superior, but a revelation of such a matter is soon recognized or suspected by others, and sometimes the fact of disclosures becomes even generally known. As a result of this, a general opprobrium might alight upon the prefect and his office, and the succeeding classes of religious students for many years would choose to keep their problems to themselves. Many, therefore, would not receive the direction and the solution of spiritual difficulties which they would otherwise have received. Then, too, the content of the manifestation of conscience is so sacred to the individual that he is entitled to oppose strenuously any likelihood of its disclosure, unless he has the fullest assurance that absolute secrecy will be observed. The voluntary manifestation would immediately become non-extant, if even the least suspicion were attached to its inviolability. Thus, a failure to observe the secrecy so essential to the manifestation would result in fundamental and far-reaching ill effects in every religious institute.[66]

A principal difficulty against this solution comes from an analogy with other entrusted secrets. Moralists agree, for example, that a doctor

---

Review, CXXVIII (1953), pp. 200-201; Ford-Kelly, "Notes on Moral Theology, 1953," *Theological Studies*, XV (1954), pp. 83-84.

[66] Gill, *The Spiritual Prefect in Clerical Religious Houses of Study*, The Catholic University of America Canon Law Studies, n. 216 (Washington, D.C.: The Catholic University of America Press, 1954), pp. 108-110.

can warn a prospective bride if he finds that her fiance has a contagious disease which would threaten her health and future happiness.[67] Theologians also approve the practice whereby doctors are at times obliged to report bullet wounds to the police, in consideration of the principle that the common good demands exceptions even to the entrusted secret. Why does not the same hold true in the cases concerning the manifestation just outlined? While both the medical and the spiritual secrets here adduced belong to the entrusted type, the secret of the manifestation is on a higher level than its medical counterpart. The confidence which men have in their spiritual directors is more intrinsic to the common good and therefore much more inviolable than the confidence placed in doctors—though both are of course of fundamental importance. For all practical purposes, therefore, the secret of the manifestation should be kept with an inviolability just short of the confessional secret itself.

Can the superior, in the cases under discussion, use the manifestation knowledge to dismiss a subject *without revealing the secret in any way to any one?* Although theoretically a case can be conceived where a superior might with strict right use such knowledge against an individual to forfend the community from a preponderant harm, still, because of the practical impossibility of preventing the causal relationship of this course of action from entering the domain of public knowledge, there seems to be absolutely no case in which moral justification for such procedure can be offered. It cannot be too strongly urged that the element of confidence so inherent to the manifestation is not only disrupted by direct and formal revelation of knowledge so gained, but is also seriously impaired by any use of related knowledge which causes it to fall under suspicion. Often enough, in the psychology of human affairs, suspicions induce a greater degree of notoriety than any *fait accompli.*

When one considers the affinities of the manifestation of conscience and the sacrament of penance, it is no wonder that the latter's priority over all other entrusted secrets should approximate its inviolability to that of the seal of confession. Pius XI, in his encyclical letter *Ad*

[67] *Opera Moralia S. Alphonsi Mariae De Ligorio* (4 vols., Romae: Ex Typographia Vaticana, 1905-1912), n. 971,4.

Catholici sacerdotii of December 20, 1935,[68] offers confirmation of this position:

> Let Superiors of seminaries, together with the spiritual directors and confessors, reflect how weighty a responsibility they assume before God, before the Church, and before the youths themselves, if they do not take all means at their disposal to avoid a false step. We declare, too, that the confessors and spiritual directors could also be responsible for such a grave error; *not indeed because they can take any outward action, since this is severely forbidden them by their most delicate office itself, and often also by the inviolable sacramental seal;* but because they can have a great influence on the souls of individual students, and with paternal firmness they should guide each according to his spiritual needs. Should the superiors, for whatever cause, not take steps or show themselves weak, then especially should confessors and spiritual directors admonish the unsuited and unworthy, without any regard to human consideration, of their obligation to retire while yet there is time..."[69]

Pope Pius XI here highlights the sacred character of the knowledge received from confession as well as from the manifestation of conscience, and forbids the revelation of either category of knowledge, even to exclude a positively unworthy candidate from proceeding to sacred orders.

Article 3: [All Religious Superiors] "Are Strictly Forbidden to Induce in any Manner Persons Subject to Them to Make a Manifestation of Conscience to Them."

Section 1: *"Strictly Forbidden"*

The decree *Quemadmodum* used forceful expressions in prohibiting the elicited manifestation of conscience. Its opening norm, for instance, reads:

> His Holiness annuls, abrogates, and declares of no force whatever all regulations whatever in the constitutions... in this point in which these constitutions regard the secret manifestation of conscience in whatsoever manner or under what means soever.[70]

A later section of the decree is more specific and parallels canon 530, §1, in meaning:

> He [His Holiness], moreover, forbids absolutely such Superiors, male and female, no matter what may be their rank and eminence,

[68] *AAS*, XXVIII (1936), 5-53.

[69] *The Catholic Mind*, XXXIV (1936), pp. 69-70 (emphasis supplied).

[70] *Fontes*, n. 2017; Sabetti, *The Decree*, p. 11.

> from endeavoring, directly or indirectly, . . . to induce their subjects to make to them any such manifestation of conscience.[71]

The phrase *strictly forbidden* of canon 530, §1, is an expression equal in forcefulness to the language of the decree. The recent law for Oriental Religious in canon 62 phrased its prohibition on the matter thus: "All religious superiors are severely forbidden (*severe vetantur*) . . . to induce the manifestation of conscience." This language points to the unwavering attitude of the Church on the seriousness of the matter involved.

The clarity of the language of these laws has induced unanimity among commentators that this prohibition binds under mortal sin.[72] Nevertheless, all are in agreement that the law allows of lightness of matter. Thus, if the coercion used in eliciting a manifestation is slight, or if there is relatively unimportant matter involved, serious sin may well be absent.

Section 2: *"To Induce in any Manner"*

Again the law makes use of very broad terminology, and thereby encompasses any and every way in which one person can unduly influence another. The phrase, *to induce in any manner,* of canon 530, §1, expresses summarily the specifically detailed modalities of *Quemadmodum:*

> He [His Holiness], moreover, forbids absolutely such Superiors . . . from endeavoring, directly or indirectly, by command, counsel, fear, threats, or blandishments, to induce . . . any such manifestation of conscience.[73]

Thus, the canon repeats the verb *to induce* (*inducere*), used by the decree, but where the canon simply states *in any manner* (*quoquo modo*), the decree has specified further *directly or indirectly, by command, counsel, intimidation* . . . This enumeration of modalities, however, retains all its interpretative force, since the canon in effect succinctly reiterates the more leisurely elaboration of the decree.

Superiors are forbidden to induce subjects by moral force to manifest their consciences to them. They may not, for example, show a marked

[71] *Fontes, loc. cit.;* Sabetti, *The Decree,* p. 13.

[72] Schaefer, *De Religiosis,* p. 365, n. 687; Larraona, "Commentarium Codicis," *CpR,* XII (1931), p. 127; Voltas, "De Aperienda," *CpR,* I, (1920), p. 148.

[73] *Fontes,* n. 2017; Sabetti, *The Decree,* p. 13.

preference for those of their subjects who freely and spontaneously give them an account of their interior life, nor may they treat with aloofness those subjects who refrain from giving such a manifestation. The superiors must refrain from taking the initiative with their subordinates and thus exerting any kind of undue influence. They must certainly abstain from using any kind of intimidation or threat, and must not show themselves offended or suspicious with regard to those subjects who prefer an attitude of reserve. Superiors may by no means impose upon these subjects restrictions or punishments, however light, unless there are other solid foundations for these.

Finally, it must be noted that at times the superior will be able to take the first step without inducing the manifestation in the sense meant by the law. If a superior notices a subject who is in a state of sadness or trouble, he may inquire discreetly and delicately as to the cause. Such inquiries could, in fact, be an obligation of charity. But he must be cautious not to insist if he sees that the subject prefers not to explain the causes of his melancholy.[74] In a word, it is the will of the legislator that this delicate practice of manifesting one's conscience to a superior be always characterized by the utmost freedom and spontaneity.

Section 3: *"The Persons Subject to Them."*

There is no doubt that the canon includes professed religious and novices by the phrase *persons subject to them*. The professed are encompassed by virtue of their vows. Novices are subjects in a broad but proper sense according to the norm of canon 561, §2, which accords the master of novices authority over them. It is also clear that the words in question include women religious with regard to their regular superiors.[75] Authors are in agreement up to this point.[76]

Some doubt arises, however, with regard to postulants. Vermeersch-Creusen, for example, are of the opinion that postulants are not included within the scope of the phrase *persons subject to them*.[77]

[74]Creusen-Ellis, *Religious Men and Women*, n. 131.

[75]Schaefer, *De Religiosis*, p. 366, n. 689.

[76]Schaefer, *De Religiosis*, p. 366, n. 689; Larraona, "Commentarium Codicis," *CpR*, XII (1931), 127; Voltas, "De Aperienda," *CpR*, I (1920), 148; Vermeersch-Creusen, *Epitome*, n. 650; Ellis, "Superiors and Manifestation of Conscience," *Review for Religious*, II (1943), 104.

[77]*Epitome*, I, n. 650.

No. 81 of the Norms of 1940 employs the terms *sisters subject to them* and *religious subjects.* These terms are obviously more restricted than the phrase *persons subject to them* of the canon and could indicate a change of mind in the legislator. None the less, the only three legal enactments on the subject of the manifestation, i.e., *Quemadmodum* of 1890, canon 530 of the Code, and canon 62 of the Law for Oriental Religious of 1952, all use the same broad term, *persons subject to them.* The use and retention of such broad terminology indicates that the legislator intended to include as many subjects as possible. While postulants certainly are not religious, they are *persons subject* to their respective superiors and directors, and therefore fall under the protection extended by the present law. This view is expressly endorsed by a number of noteworthy commentators.[78]

Professed religious, novices, and postulants were the only persons who had been bound by the Rules, constitutions, and directories which prior to *Quemadmodum* had prescribed the manifestation of conscience. These alone had forfeited the natural right of the sanctuary of conscience; these alone, therefore, were in need of a positive law to restore and safeguard the freely surrendered natural right which had been abused. Therefore, it does not seem necessary to extend the protection of canon 530 beyond the professed, novices and the postulants, because all other subjects (e.g., tertiaries, candidates, minor seminarians, domestics, transients)[79] still remained in possession of a natural right which they had never relinquished.

Section 4: *"To Make to Them."*

The fore-cited words are another instance where the canon reiterates *Quemadmodum*. Canon 62 of the Law for Oriental Religious retains the identical wording. Larraona points out how the preparatory outlines of the Code provisionally embodied the prohibition to elicit a manifestation with respect to persons distinct from the elicitor.[80] Thus the outlines of 1914 read: "to make it [the manifestation of con-

[78]Schaefer, *De Religiosis,* p. 366, n. 689; Larraona, "Commentarium Codicis," *CpR,* XII (1931), 127; Ellis, "Superiors and Manifestation of Conscience," *Review for Religious,* II (1943), 104; Voltas, "De Aperienda," *CpR,* I (1920), 148.

[79]Cf. canon 514, §1.

[80]"Commentarium Codicis," *CpR,* XII (1931), 128.

science] to themselves or to other superiors."[81] The outlines of 1916 had an even more extensive reading: "to make it [the manifestation of conscience] to themselves or to others."[82] These broader tentative formulas, however, were not retained.

The words used by the canon are clear. The only thing forbidden is for a superior to elicit that the manifestation be made to himself. Superiors are free to counsel and recommend that their subjects make a manifestation to other superiors, to confessors, to spiritual directors. Similarly, preachers and retreat masters can expound on the benefits of the manifestation and recommend its use to religious subjects.

Larraona, sensing possible abuses as a result of having one superior suggest that a manifestation be made to another superior, wisely points out that the law should not be frustrated by fraud and circumvention.[83] Finally, as should be evident, all use of force and constraint is out of the question even in this instance.

Section 5: [*To Make*] *"A Manifestation of Conscience."*

As was seen in the preceding chapter,[84] by the term *manifestation of conscience* the law meant a revelation of intimate matters of heart and conscience. The law prohibits all such revelations in any and all obligatory forms or guises. Thus, following the divisions offered above,[85] the present law rules out the elicited quasi-sacramental manifestation with its material object of sins, faults and imperfections, no less than the elicited ascetical manifestation having for its object hidden virtues, special graces, and illuminations, on the one hand, and temptations, propensities to evil, and personal repugnances, on the other.

[81] "Sibi aut aliis superioribus peragendam."—*Loc. cit.*

[82] "Sibi aut aliis peragendam."—*Loc. cit.*

[83] "Commentarium Codicis," *CpR,* XII (1931), 128.

[84] Cf. *supra,* pp. 51-54.

[85] Cf. *loc. cit.*

CHAPTER VI

COMMENTARY ON §2 OF CANON 530

The text of canon 530, §2, reads: "Subjects, however, are not forbidden freely and spontaneously to open their souls to their superiors; indeed it is expedient that they approach their superiors with filial confidence, and if the superiors are priests, reveal to them the doubts and anxieties of their conscience." The present chapter will consider in detail the various components of this juridical unit.

ARTICLE 1: "SUBJECTS, HOWEVER, ARE NOT FORBIDDEN FREELY AND SPONTANEOUSLY TO OPEN THEIR SOULS TO THEIR SUPERIORS."

These opening words of §2, are an almost verbatim reiteration of *Quemadmodum,* which reads: "This, however, in nowise hinders subjects from freely and of their own accord opening their hearts to their superiors..."[1] Thus, it is clear from both the decree and the canon itself that the lawmaker did not intend to interdict the manifestation of conscience as such, but only to legislate against its solicited and obligatory form. Commenting on this section of the decree, Pius De Langogne wrote:

> To those who, in view of the proscriptions and prescriptions of the Holy See, were, from the very first, uneasy about hierarchical subordination, the training of novices, and the spiritual helps which the religious gained from their Superiors, the third decree will give full satisfaction. Why, men of little faith, why do you fear that the wisdom of the Church has lost its prudence? The paternal solicitude of our august Pontiff for 'this chosen portion of his flock,' as says the Decree, has known how to repress abuse without touching the hierarchy, to cut off the sprouts without damaging the same, without stopping or lessening its vivifying action.
>
> Today, as heretofore, inferiors and Superiors have reciprocal rights and duties, proper attention to which will be for Religious Communities a practical form of filial confidence and paternal devotion.
>
> This does not prevent subjects from opening their hearts freely and spontaneously to Superiors for the purpose of receiving prudent

[1] *Fontes,* n. 2017; Sabetti, *The Decree,* p. 14.

counsel and direction in their doubts and anxieties, for the acquisition of virtues and progress in perfection.[2]

The expression *freely and spontaneously* in the phrase under consideration simply means that any manifestation must be entered upon and take its initiative from the subject making it. There is to be no contrivance or constraint of any kind on the part of the superior. Freedom of conscience is a delicate and difficult matter. §1 protects this freedom by prohibiting superiors to induce the manifestation of conscience from their subjects. §2 implies this prohibition by stating that every manifestation must be characterized by freedom and spontaneity of initiative.

The phrase *subjects are not forbidden to open their souls to their superiors* signalizes the voice of the Church distinctly guaranteeing the natural right of every man to confide in whomsoever he may deem worthy to share the confidences of his soul. The jurisprudence of the decades just prior to the decree inhibited even the free and spontaneous manifestation owing to the abuses which existed at the time.[3] Both *Quemadmodum* and the Code, however, saw fit to give unreserved sanction to the free and spontaneous manifestation. Hence the broadness of terminology, *subjects are not forbidden to open their souls to their superiors.*

It is true that a later phrase in this second paragraph of canon 530 actually encourages subjects to be open with superiors who are priests as to "doubts and anxieties of conscience." Should this be understood as qualifying and limiting the opening expression of the paragraph which in unrestricted terms refers to all superiors? Motives of prudence may in concrete instances demand that subjects reserve delicate matters of conscience for priests, but, juridically speaking, this reservation is not evidently warranted by the broad language of the law. As Huysmans remarks, "The text of the law does not admit of any restriction: 'not prohibited' and 'to open their souls' are vague and general expressions which correspond completely to the exigencies of the natural law."[4] By the same token, prudence will at times dictate to the lay superior

[2]*Manifestation of Conscience*, pp. 74-75.

[3]"The manifestation of conscience is restricted to public transgressions of the rule and to progress in the virtues, and it is to be facultative, not obligatory."—*Analecta Iuris Pontificii*, VI (1861), 1052.

[4]*La Manifestation de Conscience en Religion*, p. 109.

to refer his subject to his confessor. It should be emphasized that the liberty here afforded the subject in nowise dispenses him from using an adequate measure of discretion, especially when manifesting intimate secrets to lay superiors.

ARTICLE 2: "INDEED IT IS EXPEDIENT THAT THEY [SUBJECTS] APPROACH THEIR SUPERIORS WITH FILIAL CONFIDENCE."

This instruction or direction again refers to all superiors, both clerical and lay. Voltas discovers in this disposition of the canon a certain fear on the part of the legislator that the strong and severe animadversions of the particular responses of the last century, that *Quemadmodum,* and §1 of this canon might cause or occasion subjects to forfeit some of the love, reverence, obedience and respect which is due to their superiors.[5] The present recommendation by the legislator is clearly aimed at precluding any such loss of confidence in superiors. More, the affirmative cast of its exhortation, no less than the choice of terms (e.g., "it is expedient," "approach," "filial") is implicitly expressive of the legislator's mind that it would be deeply regretable for subjects not to place duly reverent trust in their superiors.

Beyond a doubt there should exist between subject and superior that closeness and confidence which bind parent and child in a model family. What is more desirable or natural than that a son or daughter approach either parent with complete faith in time of doubt or trial? Similarly, a religious should find an understanding counterpart in the person of his superior. Not without reason therefore are religious institutes called *families,* and the membership of the same addressed with titles evocative of genuine affection—"father," "mother," "sister," "brother." The present disposition of the Code, clearly enough, is intended as a reminder of the familial structure basic to the religious life. Hence, subjects are to have true filial confidence in their superiors, while superiors should be as fathers to their subordinates.[6]

Two further observations are in order. It should not be forgotten that the exigencies of his position thrust upon the superior the double role of sympathetic counsellor and prudent guide. In the fulfillment of both these functions, the superior often has within reach an advantage

[5] "De Aperienda," *CpR,* I (1920), p. 149.

[6] Ford, "Paternal Government and Filial Confidence in Superiors," *Review for Religious,* II (1943), p. 148.

denied the confessor, namely, a close range knowledge of the subject based upon the latter's over-all, daily, external conduct.[7]

It is no less important to recall that the recommendation made by the said paragraph must be taken in context. Accordingly, the disposition at hand does not refer to filial confidence in some vague or tenuous way, but in conjunction with the manifestation of conscience. Larraona observes appropriately that to limit this recommendation of the law to some intermittent display of affection or to some kind of general openness rather than to the manifestation itself is to neglect the contextual bearing of the law and to restrict its object artificially.[8]

That this portion of the Canon enlarges upon the opening, negative disposition of §2, cannot be gainsaid. Not only, therefore, is it not forbidden for a religious to make a manifestation to his superior, but it can even be an expedient thing to do, provided always that the subject is acting freely and spontaneously.

Article 3: "And if the superiors are priests, [it is expedient for subjects to] reveal to them the doubts and anxieties of their conscience."

The recommendation to reveal doubts and anxieties of conscience to priest superiors has been introduced by the Code. One purpose may well have been to forestall any undue and exaggerated reserve on the part of subjects, in view of the strict language of the laws condemning the obligatory and elicited manifestation of conscience.[9] Another reason for this particular addition is, of course, the fact that the canon is addressed to all religious, clerics included, whereas *Quemadmodum* was directed only to lay religious.

The first two dispositions of the second paragraph of canon 530 had reference to all superiors; the present norm applies only to priest superiors. This final unit of canon 530 will be discussed under two headings:

Section 1: The Superiors in Question
Section 2: The Matter in Question.

[7]Ellis, "Superiors and Manifestation of Conscience," *Review for Religious,* II (1943), p. 105.

[8]"Commentarium Codicis," *CpR,* XII (1931), p. 129, note (428).

[9]Voltas, "De Aperienda," *CpR,* I (1920), p. 149.

Section 1: *The Superiors in Question*

From a positive standpoint, the legal import of this concluding portion of the canon is immediately clear. Subjects are instructed as to the advisability of being open with priest superiors even as regards ***doubts and anxieties of conscience.*** The purpose for this recommendation as also for the distinction here between clerical and lay superiors stems from the likelihood that such an intimate manifestation will be fruitful by reason of the priest superior's scientific training in ascetico-moral theology. By way of general rule, the same cannot be said of lay superiors. The law here regards the priest as the trained director of souls and the representative of the Master of the spiritual life. Hence its inference that he, more than anyone else, should prove the most prudent and sympathetic of counsellors to those confiding their problems to him.[10] This disposition applies not only to clerical religious with reference to their superiors, but also to lay religious who are governed by priests, e.g., the Order of St. John of God.[11] It likewise applies to nuns in relation to their regular superiors.

From a negative point of view, on the other hand, there is no immediate clarity because the question of superiors in the present disposition is neither clearly nor completely determined. Religious subjects, obviously enough, are not encouraged to manifest their ***doubts and anxieties of conscience*** to lay superiors, whereas they are so encouraged with reference to priest superiors. The question arises: Is this non-encouragement to be interpreted in terms of a prohibition?

Voltas answers in the affirmative on the premise that lay men and women lack the knowledge and discretion necessary to handle with competence not only ***doubts and anxieties of conscience*** relating to sin, but also allied problems.[12] Coronata, much more moderate in his judgment, merely indicates that it is not suitable to reveal one's doubts and anxieties of conscience to superioresses or to lay superiors.[13] For all this, it must be pointed out that in a strict juridical context the mere non-recommendation of a practice is not the equivalent of desig-

10Ellis, "Superiors and the Manifestation of Conscience," *Review for Religious,* II (1943), p. 106.

11Voltas, "De Aperienda," *CpR,* I (1920), p. 150.

12"De Aperienda," *CpR,* I (1920), p. 150.

13*Institutiones Iuris Canonici,* I, p. 676, note 5.

nating it as universally unfit—much less is it tantamount to condemning it altogether.[14]

The blanket judgment that all lay superiors are unfit spiritual directors is patently false. St. Benedict, St. Francis of Assisi, St. Theresa of Avila may be readily instanced. In view of this likelihood the Church by her silence has here presumably adapted a prudent reserve. She has neither recommended nor forbidden the making of this intimate, spontaneous manifestation to lay superiors, preferring to leave the decision in each particular case to the prudent judgment of the subject and superior in question. The law seems to envision instances where intimate manifestations to lay superiors will prove useful; hence its prudent disinclination to condemn this practice. At the same time the law foresees many instances in which such manifestations could prove useless and even harmful; hence its prudent refusal to commend this practice. A religious brother or sister need not, therefore, reproach himself with lack of confidence if he prefers to reserve the manifestation of his difficulties of conscience to his confessor or priest spiritual director.[15] Nevertheless, it sometimes happens that the best advice on a given matter can come from a lay superior because of his more ample and direct knowledge of the subject. For this reason the law does not prohibit subjects from opening their consciences to lay superiors.

To summarize, the Code does not forbid religious to make a manifestation of doubts and troubles of conscience to a lay superior. By the same token, it refrains from pronouncing on the general advisability of so doing, as in fact, it does in the case of superiors signed with the priestly character.[16]

Section 2: The Matter in Question

The final point to be considered in this commentary on canon 530 is the precise meaning of the words ***doubts and anxieties of conscience.*** Their importance can be surmised from the fact that they provide the only basis for the different course of action here recommended. Subjects are encouraged to manifest such matters to priest superiors; they

[14] Huysmans, *La Manifestation de Conscience en Religion*, p. 111; Ellis, "Superiors and Manifestation of Conscience," *Review for Religious*, II (1943), p. 106.

[15] Creusen-Ellis, *Religious Men and Women*, n. 132.

[16] Creusen-Ellis, *Religious Men and Women*, n. 132.

are not so encouraged as regards lay superiors. This distinction, necessitated by the very nature of the matter involved, indicates with sufficient accuracy what the law intends to include under the phrase *doubts and anxieties of conscience.*

This phrase includes, apart from doubts and perplexities about sin as such, all questions of conscience which because of their difficulty, importance, or uncertainty, require the help of one who has been trained in moral and ascetical theology.[17] Schaefer subscribes to this broad interpretation of the words in question and would extend them to include sins committed in the past and cases of conscience.[18] Voltas says that the words *doubts and anxieties of conscience* refer not only to doubts and anxieties touching upon sins, but also to many other cases for the solution of which lay superiors lack the required theological knowledge.[19] Consequently, the amplitude of the phrase, *doubts and anxieties of conscience,* warrants inclusion of all cases where the ascetico-moral training of the priest superior qualifies him as a more competent guide than the lay superior who generally lacks such formation.

In conclusion, §1 of canon 530 strictly forbids the elicited manifestation of conscience; §2 in no way mitigates this prohibition. It merely tempers the rigor of the foregoing prohibition and removes the basis for an overly strict interpretation which would destroy the proper close relationship which should obtain between superior and subject. It is not correct, therefore, to affirm that the Church has condemned the manifestation of conscience as such, for her intention does not extend beyond a just and prudent desire to outlaw all contrivance and constraint with reference to the manifestation of conscience. The Church readily appreciates the multiple values in a free and spontaneous manifestation of conscience: §2 of canon 530 gives official expression to that recognition.

[17]Ellis, "Superiors and the Manifestation," *Review for Religious,* II (1943), p. 106.

[18]*De Religiosis,* p. 367, n. 691.

[19]"De Aperienda," *CpR,* I (1920), p. 150. Even the opinion of Larraona, who points out that the interpretation of *doubts and anxieties of conscience* should not be overly extended, is in reality quite broad. Cf. "Commentarium Codicis," *CpR,* XII (1931), p. 130, note (431).

CONCLUSIONS

1. The manifestation of conscience may be considered co-terminous with the beginnings of the religious life itself. (pp. 1-19)

2. The writings of St. Bonaventure contain the first reference to the use of knowledge gained from the manifestation, in the external government of the religious community. (pp. 21-22)

3. The manifestation of conscience attained full crystallization through the efforts of St. Ignatius of Loyola and the early legislators of the Society of Jesus. (pp. 22-30)

4. Although anticipated by particular responses issued by the Sacred Congregation of Bishops and Regulars, the decree *Quemadmodum* of 1890 embodies the first comprehensive effort of the common law to come to grips with the practical problems centering around the manifestation of conscience. (pp. 34-37)

5. *Quemadmodum* has lost all its juridic force, but retains its importance as an interpretative source for canon 530. (pp. 43-46)

6. The two basic norms of *Quemadmodum* regarding the manifestation of conscience—the prohibition imposed upon superiors, and the option extended to subordinates—are reproduced by canon 530. (pp. 44-46)

7. By dividing its broad material object, one may distinguish the manifestation into three separate categories: the quasi-sacramental, the ascetical, and the academic manifestations. (pp. 51-54)

8. The expression *all religious superiors* of canon 530 refers to superiors in a broad sense of the word. Therefore, the prohibition of canon 530 extends not only to superiors properly so-called, but also to masters of novices, prefects of students, and similar officials with at least social or domestic power in the external life of the community. (pp. 55-71)

9. When a superior, or an official with power in the external government of the community, urges or exhorts that subjects manifest themselves to him, he is employing moral force. (p. 60)

10. In practice a confidence received for the sake of spiritual direction through the manifestation of conscience may never be revealed. In practice a confidence received for the sake of spiritual direction through the manifestation may never be used. (pp. 72-77)

11. The prohibition of canon 530 against inducing the manifestation binds under pain of grave sin, but admits of lightness of matter. (pp. 77-78)

12. The phrase *persons subject to them* of canon 530 includes those categories of subjects who prior to *Quemadmodum* had surrendered their liberty of conscience by embracing Rules or constitutions which demanded the making of the manifestation. (pp. 79-80)

13. Canon 530, §2, permits subjects to make the manifestation of conscience to all superiors. It encourages subjects to make the manifestation of conscience, exclusive of doubts and anxieties of conscience, to all superiors. It encourages subjects to make the manifestation of conscience, inclusive of doubts and anxieties of conscience, solely to priest superiors. (pp. 82-88)

APPENDIX

Decree

of the Sacred Congregation of Bishops and Regulars on the prohibition of the manifestation of conscience, and on the rights of confessors with respect to religious women and the Institutes of Lay Men.*

(Official translation)

"Just as it is the fate of human beings, how praiseworthy and holy soever they may be in themselves, even so is it of laws wisely enacted, to be liable to be misused and perverted to purposes opposed and foreign to their nature. Wherefore it sometimes happens that they no longer serve the purposes which the lawmakers had in view; nay, they sometimes even produce quite a contrary result.

"Much it is to be deplored that such has proved to be the case with the laws of several Congregations, Societies, and Institutes, both of women who emit simple or solemn vows, and of men who by their profession and discipline are merely laymen. For, inasmuch as occasionally their Constitutions permitted the making of a manifestation of conscience, in order that thereby the members might the more easily learn, in their doubts, from experienced Superiors, how to walk in the path of perfection, it has happened, on the contrary, that some of the latter have introduced the practice of thoroughly inquiring into the state of their subjects' conscience, which is a thing reserved exclusively to the Sacrament of Penance. In like manner, and in conformity with the prescriptions of the Sacred Canons, it was ordered that Sacramental Confession in all such communities should be made to the respective Ordinary and Extraordinary Confessors; while, on the other hand, the arbitrary conduct of some Superiors has gone so far as to refuse to their subjects an Extraordinary Confessor, even in cases where the conscience of the person so refused stood greatly in need of such a privilege. These Superiors were given a rule of discretion and prudence for the purpose of enabling them to direct their subjects in a proper and right use of peculiar penitential exercises and other practices of piety; but this very rule, also, was so perverted by abuse that they [the Superiors] took it on themselves to permit, at their pleasure, their subjects to approach the Holy Table, or even sometimes to forbid them Communion altogether. Hence it has happened that such regulations as these, established for the salutary and wise purpose of promoting the spiritual progress of members and fostering in communities the

*Translation from Sabetti, *The Decree "Quemadmodum," with Explanations* (Baltimore: John Murphy & Co., 1892)

union growing out of peace and concord, have not unfrequently resulted in imperilling the salvation of souls, in deeply disturbing consciences, and, moreover, in the disturbance of exterior peace,—as it is most evidently proved by the appeals and complaints frequently made to the Holy See.

"Wherefore our Most Holy Father, Leo XII., [*sic*] impelled by the peculiar solicitude for which he is distinguished toward the most select portion of his flock, in the audience which he gave me, the Cardinal-Prefect of the Sacred Congregation of Bishops and Regulars, on the 14th day of December, 1890, after carefully and diligently considering everything, has willed, determined, and decreed as follows:

"His Holiness annuls, abrogates, and declares of no force whatever, hereafter, all regulations whatsoever in the Constitutions of Pious Societies and Institutes of women who emit either simple or solemn vows, as well as in those of men of the purely lay order (even though the said constitutions should have received from the Holy See approbation in any form soever, even that which is termed most special), in this one point, in which these Constitutions regard the secret manifestation of conscience in whatsoever manner or under what name soever. He therefore seriously enjoins on all the Superiors, Male and Female, of such Institutes, Congregations, and Societies to absolutely cancel and expunge altogether from their respective Constitutions, Directories, and Manuals all the aforesaid regulations. Likewise he declares whatsoever usages and customs in this matter, even such as are from time out of mind, to be null and void and to be abolished.

"He, moreover, forbids absolutely such Superiors, male and female, no matter what may be their rank and eminence, from endeavoring, directly or indirectly, by command, counsel, fear, threats, or blandishments, to induce their subjects to make to them any such manifestation of conscience; and he commands these subjects on their part to denounce to the higher Superiors such as dare to induce them to make such manifestation; and if the guilty one be the Superior-General the denunciation should by them be made to this Sacred Congregation.

"This, however, in nowise hinders subjects from freely and of their own accord opening their hearts to their Superiors, for the purpose of obtaining from their prudence, counsel and direction, in doubts and perplexities, in order to aid them in acquiring virtues and advancing in perfection.

"Moreover, while the prescriptions of the Holy Council of Trent, Sess. 25, Cap. 10, de Regul., retain their full vigor, as well as the decrees of Benedict XIV. of holy memory in the Constitution *Pastoralis Curae,* His Holiness admonishes Prelates and Superiors not to deny their subjects an Extraordinary Confessor as often as the need of their conscience requires it, and without seeking to find out in any way the reason why their subjects make such a demand, or without showing that they resent it. And, lest so provident a disposition as this should be made illusory, he exhorts the Ordinaries to name, in all localities of their diocese, in which there are communities of women, well-qualified priests with the necessary faculties, to whom such Religious may easily have recourse to receive the Sacrament of Penance.

"As to what regards either permission or prohibition to receive Holy Communion, His Holiness also decrees that such permission or prohibition belongs solely to the Ordinary or Extraordinary Confessor, the Superiors having no right whatever to interfere in the matter, save only the case in which any one of their subjects had given scandal to the community since his or her last confession, or had been guilty of some grievous public fault, and this only until the guilty one had once more received the Sacrament of Penance.

"And all are hereby admonished to prepare themselves diligently and to approach Holy Communion on the days prescribed in their respective Rules; and when the Confessor may judge conducive to the spiritual advancement of any member to receive more frequently, he may give the needful permission. But whoever receives from the Confessor the permission to receive more frequent or daily Communion is bound to inform the Superior of the same; should the latter think that he has just and serious reasons to oppose such frequent Communion, he is bound to make them known to the Confessor, in whose judgment he must absolutely acquiesce.

"His Holiness, furthermore, commands all Superiors General, Provincials, and Local Superiors of the Institutes aforementioned, whether of men or of women, to observe zealously and accurately the regulations prescribed in this Decree under pain of incurring ipso facto the penalties decreed against Superiors who violate the mandates of the Holy See.

"He lastly commands that copies of this present Decree, translated into the vernacular, shall be inserted in the Constitutions of the said pious Institutes, and that at least once in a twelvemonth, at a stated time in each House, either in the public Refectory, or in Chapter assembled for this special purpose, this Decree shall be read in a loud and intelligible voice.

"And thus hath His Holiness determined and decreed, notwithstanding all things to the contrary, even such as are worthy of special and individual mention."

Given at Rome from the Secretariate of the said Sacred Congregation of Bishops and Regulars, the 17th day of December, 1890.

I. Card. Verga, *Prefect,*
Fr. Aloysius Episc. Callinicen., *Secretary.*

BIBLIOGRAPHY

Sources

Acta Apostolicae Sedis, Commentarium Officiale, Romae, 1909—

Acta Sanctae Sedis, 41 vols., Romae, 1865-1908.

Analecta Iuris Pontificii, Romae, Parisiis, 1855-1890.

Apostolic Constitution "Sedes Sapientiae and the General Statutes," Sole Official English text), Washington, D.C.: The Catholic University of America Press, 1957.

Codex Iuris Canonici Pii X Pontificis Maximi iussu digestus Benedicti Papae XV auctoritate promulgatus, Romae: Typis Polyglottis Vaticanis, 1917.

Codicis Iuris Canonici Fontes cura Emi Petri Card. Gasparri editi, 9 vols., Romae, [later Civitate Vaticana]: Typis Polyglottis Vaticanis, 1923-1939. (Vols. VII-IX, ed. *cura et studio Emi Iustiniani Card. Seredi.*)

Collectanea in usum secretariae S. Congregationis Episcoporum et Regularium, ed. A. Bizzarri, Romae, 1885.

Elenchus quaestionum quibus a Religionibus et Societatibus in Relatione ad S. Sedem quinto quoquo anno transmittenda respondendum est ad normam Decreti "Cum transactis," Romae: Typis Polyglottis Vaticanis, 1949.

Institutiones Societatis Jesu, 3 vols., Florentiae: Typographia a SS. Conceptione, 1892-1893.

Motu Proprio, de Religiosis . . . pro Ecclesiis Orientalibus, Romae: Typis Polyglottis Vaticanis, 1952.

Normae pro constitutionibus congregationum Iuris diocescani a S.C. de Propaganda Fide dependentium, Romae: Typis Polyglottis Vaticanis, 1940.

Normae Secundum Quas S. Congre. Episcoporum et Regularium Procedere Solet in Approbandis Novis Institutis Votorum Simplicium, Romae, 1901.

Oxford Dictionary of the Christian Church, The, London: Oxford University Press, 1957.

Authors

Aertnys, J.-Damen, C.A., *Theologia Moralis secundum doctrinam S. Alfonsi de Liguori Doct. Ecclesiae,* 13 ed., 2 vols., Romae: Marietti, 1939.

Alt, Vigilius, *De Potestate Magistri Spiritus ad normam C.* 588, Romae: Officium Libri Catholici, 1949.

Augustine, Charles, *A Commentary on the New Code of Canon Law,* 8 vols., St. Louis: B. Herder Book Co., 1925-1938.

Baker, Augustine, *Holy Wisdom,* Burns and Oates: London, [ ].

Bartoli, D., *Della Vita e dell'Istituto di S. Ignatio* [sic] *Fondatore della Compagnia di Giesu* [sic] *Libri Cinque,* Roma, 1650.

Bastien, Pierre, *Directoire Canonique a l'Usage des Congregations a Voeux Simples,* 4 ed., Bruges, 1933.

Berutti, Christophorus, *Institutiones Iuris Canonici,* 6 vols., Vol. III, Taurini-Romae: Marietti, 1936.

Beste, Udalricus, *Introductio in Codicem,* 2 ed., Collegeville, Minn.: St. John's Abbey Press, 1944.

Biederlack, Josephus-Fuehrich, Maximilianus, *De Religiosis,* Oeniponte, 1919.

Bonaventure, St., *Doctoris Seraphici S. Bonaventurae S.R.E. Episcopi Cardinalis Opera Omnia,* 10 vols., Ad Aquas Claras: Typographia Collegii S. Bonaventurae, 1882-1902.

Butler, Cuthbert, *Benedictine Monachism,* New York: Longmans, Greene and Co., 1924.

.................., *Sancti Benedicti Regula Monasteriorum, Editio Critico-Practica,* 2 ed., Friburgi Brisgoviae: Herder, 1927.

Cappello, Felix, *Summa Iuris Canonici in Usum Scholarum Concinnata,* 3 vols., 3 ed., Romae: apud Aedes Universitatis Gregorianae, 1938-1948.

Chelodi, Ioannes-Ciprotti, Pius, *Ius Canonicum de Personis,* 3 ed., Vicenza: Società Anonima Tipografica, 1942.

Cicognani, Amleto, *Canon Law,* 2 ed., Revised, English version by J. O'Hara and F. Brennan, Westminster, Maryland: Newman Press, 1949, Reprint of 2 ed., Philadelphia: The Dolphin Press, 1935.

Clancy, Patrick, *The Local Religious Superior,* The Catholic University of America Canon Law Studies, n. 175, Washington, D.C.: The Catholic University of America Press, 1943.

Cocchi, Guidus, *Commentarium in Codicem Iuris Canonici,* 8 vols., Taurinorum Augustae: Marietti, Vol. III, 4 ed., 1940; Vol. IV, 3 ed., 1932.

Conte a Coronata, Matthaeus, *Institutiones Iuris Canonici,* 5 vols., Vol. I, 4 ed., Taurini: Marietti, 1950.

Creusen, Josephus, *De Iuridica Status Religiosi Evolutione Synopsis Historica,* altera editio, Romae: Apud Aedes Pont. Univ. Gregorianae, 1948.

Creusen, Joseph - Ellis, Adam, *Religious Men and Women in Church Law,* 6 ed., Milwaukee: Bruce, 1957.

Delatte, P., *Commentary on the Rule of Saint Benedict,* New York: Benziger Brothers, 1921.

Fanfani, Ludovicus, *De Iure Religiosorum ad Normam Codicis Iuris Canonici,* 3 ed., Rovigo: Istituto Padano di Arti Grafiche, 1949.

Freriks, Celestine, *Religious Congregations in their External Relations,* The Catholic University of America Canon Law Studies, n. 1, Washington, D.C.: The Catholic University of America, 1916.

Gerster a Zeil, Thomas, *Ius Religiosorum,* Taurini: Marietti, 1935.

Gill, Nicholas, *The Spiritual Prefect in Clerical Religious Houses of Study,* The Catholic University of America Canon Law Studies, n. 216, Washington, D.C.: The Catholic University of America Press, 1945.

Goyeneche, S., *Quaestiones Canonicae de Iure Religiosorum,* Neapoli: M. D'Auria Pontificius Editor, 1954.

Holstensius, Lucas, et Brockie, Marianus, *Codex Regularum Monasticarum et Canonicarum,* 6 vols., Augustae Vindelicorum: Vieth, 1759.

Hurter, H., *Nomenclator Literarius Theologiae Catholicae,* 3 ed., 6 vols., Oeniponte: Libreria Academica Wagneriana, 1903-1913.

Huysmans, Francisco, *La Manifestation de Conscience en Religion*, Lovanii: Bibliotheca Alphonsiana, 1953.

Knowles, David, *The Monastic Order in England*, Cambridge: The University Press, 1940.

Korth, Francis, *The Evolution of Manifestation of Conscience in Religious Rules (III-XVI Centuries)*, Rome: Gregorian University, 1949.

Langogne, Pius de, *L'Ouverture de Conscience, les Confessions et Communions dans les Communautes*, Paris, 1891.

......................., *Manifestation of Conscience*, 2 ed., New York: Benziger Brothers, 1892.

Ligorio, S. Alphonsus de, *Opera Moralia S. Alphonsi Mariae De Ligorio*, 4 vols., Romae: Ex Typographia Vaticana, 1905-1912.

Lover, James, *The Master of Novices*, The Catholic University of America Canon Law Studies, No. 254, Washington, D.C.: The Catholic University of America Press, 1947.

Michiels, Gommarus, *Normae Generales Juris Canonici*, 2 ed., 2 vols., Parisiis, Tornaci-Romae, 1949.

Maroto, Philippus, *Institutiones Iuris Canonici ad Normam Novi Codicis*, 2 vols., Matriti, 1918-1919.

McCormick, Robert, *Confessors of Religious*, The Catholic University of America Canon Law Studies, No. 33, Washington, D.C.: Catholic University of America, 1926.

Migne, J. P., *Patrologiae Cursus Completus, Series Graeca*, 161 vols., Parisiis, 1856-1866.

..........................., *Patrologiae Cursus Completus, Series Latina*, 221 vols., Parisiis, 1844-1864.

Noldin, H. - Schmitt, A. - Heinzel, G. *Summa Theologiae Moralis*, 31 ed., 3 vols., Oeniponte: Typis et Sumptibus Feliciani Rauch, 1957.

Pejska, Josephus, *Ius Canonicum Religiosorum*, 3 ed., Friburgi Brisgoviae: Herder, 1927.

Piatus Montensis, *Praelectiones Iuris Regularium*, 3 ed., 3 vols., Tournay: Casterman, 1906.

Regatillo, Eduardus, *Institutiones Iuris Canonici*, 5 ed., 2 vols., Santander: Editorial Sal Terrae, 1956.

Rodriguez, Alphonsus, *The Practice of Christian and Religious Perfection*, 3 vols., New York: [ ].

Rose, Stuart, *Saint Ignatius of Loyola and the Early Jesuits*, London, 1891.

Ryan, John, *Irish Monasticism*, London: Longmans, Greene, and Co., 1931.

Sabetti, A., *The Decree "Quemadmodum," with Explanations*, Baltimore: John Murphy and Co., 1892.

Schaefer, Timotheus, *De Religiosis ad Normam Codicis Iuris Canonici*, 4 ed., Romae: Typis Polyglottis Vaticanis, 1947.

Schram, Dominicus, *Institutiones Theologiae Mysticae*, Augustae Vindelicorum, Matthaei, Rieger P.M. Filiorum, 1777.

Suarez, Francisco, *Opera Omnia*, 28 vols., Editio Nova a Carolo Berton, Parisiis: Apud Ludovicum Vives, 1856-1878.

Thompson, F., *Saint Ignatius of Loyola,* Burns, Oates, and Washbourne: Manchester, 1909.

Vermeersch, Arthurus - Creusen, Josephus, *Epitome Iuris Canonici,* 7 ed., 3 vols., Mechliniae-Romae: H. Dessain, 1949-1956.

Vito, Pasquale, *De Religiosis,* Napoli: Pontificia Facoltà Giuridica di Napoli, 1943.

Wernz, Franciscus - Vidal, Petrus, *Ius Canonicum,* 7 vols. in 8, Romae: Universitas Gregoriana, 1923-1938.

Ziegler, John *The Obligation of the Confessor to Instruct Penitents,* The Catholic University of America Studies in Sacred Theology (Second Series), No. 121, Washington, D.C.: The Catholic University of America Press, 1959.

ARTICLES

Anonymous, "Manifestation of Conscience and Chapter of Faults," *AER,* XX (1899), 420-421.

Arndt, A., Das Decret *Quemadmodum* fuer Ordensfrauen und Laiengenossenschaften," *Archiv fuer katholisches Kirchenrecht,* LXXVI (1896), 227-250.

Blat, Albertus, "De Potestate Superiorum in Religionibus secundum Codicem I.C." *CpR,* XVI (1935), 321-353.

Canuto, A., "De regimine domus studiorum in religione clericali exempta ad normam can. 588," *Apollinaris,* IX (1936), 19-39.

Ciprotti, P., "Adhuc de seminarii rectore an ordinariam iurisdictionem habeat ad alumnorum confessiones audiendas," *Apollinaris,* VIII (1935), 609-610.

Connell, Francis, "A Spiritual Director's Obligation of Secrecy," *AER,* CXXVIII (1953), 200-201.

Ellis, Adam, "Superiors and Manifestation of Conscience," *Review for Religious,* II (1943), 101-108.

Ford, John - Kelly, Gerald, "Notes on Moral Theology," 1953, *Theological Studies,* XV (1954), 52-102.

Ford, John, "Paternal Government and Filial Confidence in Superiors," *Review for Religious,* II (1943), 146-155.

Goyeneche, S., "Consultationes," *CpR,* I (1920), 51-52; IV (1923), 340-341; V (1924), 165-166; VI (1925), 486-491; VII (1926), 41-42; VIII (1927), 115-117; XII (1931), 254; XIII (1932), 39-40; XIV (1933), 356; *CpRM,* XVIII (1937), 90-95, 157-158; XX (1939), 18-19, 310-311; XXIII (1942), 18-21, 265-267.

Gutierrez, A., "De Manifestatione Conscientiae et Directione Spirituali in Religione," *CpRM,* XXXIV (1955), 153-174.

Kelly, Gerald, "Psychological Problems in the Religious Life," *Proceedings of the Sisters Institute of Spirituality for* 1954, Notre Dame, Ind.: University of Notre Dame Press.

Kinane, J., "The Confessor of Novices in Religious Institutes of Men," *IER,* 5 series XLI (1933), 87-88.

Langasco, Agathangelus a, "De Natura Juridica et Regimine Scholarum Internarum Religiosorum," *JP,* XVI (1936), 165-181.

.........................., "De regimine domus studiorum in religione clericali," *JP,* XVIII (1938), 118-131; XIX (1939), 55-69, 191-201.

Larraona, A., "Commentarium Codicis," *CpR,* XII (1931), 124-130.

Maroto, P., "Annotationes," *CpR,* I (1920), 106-107; III (1922), 38-44; X (1929), 334-341; *CpRM,* XVI (1935), 371-376.

Oesterle, Gerardus, "De ratione studiorum in religionibus clericalibus," *CpR,* VI (1925), 296-323.

Pius XI, "Ad Catholici Sacerdotii," *AAS,* XXVIII (1936), 5-53.

Post, John, "Novice Master's Obligations to Secrecy," *Review for Religious,* XV (1956), 11-21.

Steiger, J., "De Propagatione et Diffusione Vitae Religiosae. Synopsis Historica," *Periodica,* XIII (1924), (29)-(60); (73)-(100); (153)-(180).

Vermeersch, Arthurus, "De unitate confessarii ordinarii apud Moniales et Sorores," *Periodica,* V (1913), (1)-(12).

Voltas, Petrus, "De aperienda, directionis causa, Superioribus conscientia," *CpR,* I (1920), 83-92; 117-125; 145-151.

Periodicals

American Ecclesiastical Review, The, (formerly *Ecclesiastical Review, The,* July 1905-December, 1943), Philadelphia, 1889-1943; Washington, 1944-

Apollinaris, Romae, 1928-

Catholic Mind, The, New York, 1902-

Commentarium pro Religiosis (ab anno 1935 *Commentarium pro Religiosis et Missionariis*), Romae, 1920-

Irish Ecclesiastical Record, The, Dublin, 1864-

Jus Pontificium, Romae, 1921-1940.

Periodica de Re Canonica et Morali, utili praesertim Religiosis et Missionariis, Brugis, 1905-

Review for Religious, St. Marys, Kansas, 1942-

Theological Studies, Woodstock, Md., 1940-

Abbreviations

AAS	*Acta Apostolicae Sedis.*
AER	*American Ecclesiastical Review.*
CpR	*Commentarium pro Religiosis.*
CpRM	*Commentarium pro Religiosis et Missionariis.*
CR	*Codex Regularum.*
Fontes	*Codicis Iuris Canonici Fontes cura . . . Gasparri editi.*
IER	*Irish Ecclesiastical Record.*
JP	*Ius Pontificium.*
MPG	Migne, *Patrologia Graeca.*
MPL	Migne, *Patrologia Latina.*
Periodica	*Periodica de Re Canonica et Morali utili praesertim Religiosis et Missionariis.*

ALPHABETICAL INDEX

BIOGRAPHICAL NOTE

Dacian David Dee was born in Yonkers, New York, on June 26, 1930. He attended Sacred Heart Elementary School in that city and graduated in 1944. He then entered Glenclyffe High School, the minor seminary of the Capuchin Fathers, in Garrison, New York. After graduating in 1948 he entered the Capuchin Novitiate in Huntington, Indiana, and there pronounced his simple vows on September 1, 1949. He pursued his studies of philosophy and theology at Mary Immaculate Seminary in Garrison, New York, and was ordained to the priesthood at Sacred Heart Church in Yonkers, New York, in 1956. After completing his theological studies in 1957, he entered the School of Canon Law of the Catholic University of America, where he received the degree Baccalaureate of Canon Law in June 1958, and the degree Licentiate of Canon Law in June 1959.

CANON LAW STUDIES*

410. Dee, Rev. Dacian, O.F.M. Cap., A.B., J.C.L., The manifestation of conscience.

411. De la Cruz, Rev. Eufemio, J.C.L., The leasing of church properties in the Philippines.

412. Nessel, Rev. William, O.S.F.S., M.A., J.C.L., First amendment freedoms, papal pronouncements and concordat practice.

413. Roos, Rev. John R., M.A., S.T.L., J.C.L., The seal of confession.

414. Tierney, Rev. William J., A.B., J.C.L., Authorized ecclesiastical acts.

415. VanOmmeren, Rev. William M., J.C.L., Mental illness affecting matrimonial consent.

*For a complete list of the available numbers of this series apply to The Catholic University of America Press, 620 Michigan Ave., N.E., Washington 17, D.C., for a general catalogue.

www.ingramcontent.com/pod-product-compliance
Lightning Source LLC
LaVergne TN
LVHW050200080826
844660LV00012B/321

* 9 7 8 0 8 1 3 2 2 5 6 9 2 *